Let It Stay Between Us

A collection of letters and essays dedicated to the *Mikvah-*
(the Jewish ritual bath)

אפריון

Printed in Israel by the Worldwide Volunteer Organization *Apirion*,
which is dedicated to the popularization of *Taharas Hamishpaha*
Tel. 972-52-676-1787, (408) 7355-948 (Pacific Time)
apeeryon@gmail.com

5776-2015

Compiler and author of original Russian edition: Luba Ahuva Perlov
Initial translation to English: Devorah Shinan
Literary editor: Debbie Shapiro
Halachic consultant: Rebbetzin Tobi Hendel
Language consultant: Naomi Grossman
Cover art and layout: Luba Ahuva Perlov

   This book contains inspirational stories on the topic of *Mikvah* to inspire women to learn and to observe this *mitzvah*. From the heroism in keeping Mitzvos in soviet Russia to recent miracle stories and translations of the Rebbe's letters on *Taharas Hamishpaha*. This book is suitable for beginners and for those who are already advanced.

ISBN-13: 978-1517124946

"שישאר בינינו"
ליקטה, ערכה וכתבה את המקור ברוסית: ליבא אהובה פרלוב
תרגום ראשוני: דבורה שנאן
עיבוד ועריכה: דבי שפירא
מגיה: נעמי גרוסמן
יעוץ הלכתי: רבנית טובי הנדל
עיצוב ועטיפה -ליבא אהובה פרלוב

הודפס בארץ על ידי "אפריון",- ארגון התנדבותי להפצת טהרת המשפחה ונישואים יהודיים. סיפורי התחזקות והשראה לנשים בנושא טהרת המשפחה באנגלית. עדויות מרוסי'ה הסובטית וכן סיפורי נפלאות מתקופתינו. תרגומים מאגרות הקודש בנושא המקוה. הספר מיועד למתחילות ומתקדמות כאחת.

לעילוי נשמת
האשה החסידה הצדקנית
שמסרה נפשה על חינוך והפצת טה"מ
מרת דינה גלפרין נ"ע
בת רב אליעזר ליפמאן ויהודית לוי

לזכות משפחתה החשובה

לאריכות ימים ושנים טובות
לזכות ולרפואתו השלמה והמיידית לנכדה
חיים אליעזר ליפמאן בן דבורה לאה גלפרין שיחי"ה

Dedicated to
Dinah Halperin, of righteous memory,
daughter of Rabbi Eliezer Lipman
and Yehudis Levi.
Dinah selflessly helped and inspired
Jewish women
to return to their Jewish roots and to observe
the *Mitzvah* of *Taharas Hamishpacha*.

May her family be blessed with success and
happiness.

To the complete recovery for
Chaim Eliezer Lipman ben Dvorah Lea Galperin

৲৹

This issue of "Let It Stay Between Us" is dedicated to:

לעילוי נשמת ביילא רבקה בת אריה שמעיה ע"ה

For the elevation of the soul of
Beila Rivkah Bat Arieh Shemaya ע"ה

Table of Contents

Clear Waters

Dina[1]* and Yisrael* were born in the former Soviet Union and were a product of the Communist regime. Here is Dina's story:

I heard about *mikvah* before I left Russia. I even immersed in one prior to my wedding. But I didn't take the time to understand and appreciate this *mitzvah*. My husband-to-be wanted us to have a Jewish wedding. And as for me, I didn't see any reason not to, which is why I agreed to participate in what at that time appeared to be nothing more than a strange and archaic ritual.

Shortly after our *chuppah*, which, by the way, was amazing, my mother-in-law felt that something was not quite right with her health. Since her symptoms pointed to a serious illness, the doctor referred her for further testing. Waiting for the test results was pure torture; we were all so worried.

One evening, I had this strange, overwhelming desire to pray for my mother-in-law. I lit a candle and, with every fiber of my being, beseeched Hashem that He send her a Refuah Shleimah. I sat and stared at the lit candle as it grew shorter and shorter until it had almost disappeared. When the flame was so tiny that I thought it was about to go out, I made a fervent promise to Hashem that the moment I arrived in Israel, I would begin to keep the *mitzvah* of *Taharas Hamishpacha*, Family Purity, and in that merit my mother-in-law should regain her health!

Suddenly, the tiny flame seemed to glow and grow bigger and bigger!!! I began to cry from emotion. It

---

1   a pseudonym, in further stories asterisk (*) marks a pseudonym

was obvious to me that Hashem had accepted my prayer! Now, the flame was strong and steady. As I sat there, watching the candle burn brightly, I fell asleep.

A few days later we received wonderful news. All my mother-in-law's symptoms had disappeared. All the tests were negative!

Not long after that, we were finally able to realize our dream and move to Israel. Upon our arrival we enrolled in an *ulpan* (a Hebrew-language immigrant absorption program). Our Hebrew teacher was the first Israeli that actually communicated with us and we believed everything she said. One time she told us that a woman should never, ever, go to the *mikvah*. She described them as being "dirty, moldy and unsanitary." Today, of course, I know that she was wrong. I know that in Israel, all *mikvah*s and community pools are under government supervision and inspected regularly. A *mikvah* is more sanitary than a crowded public swimming pool, where, more often than not, people just jump in without showering. After all, before immersing in the *mikvah*, a woman must devote at least 45 minutes to her preparations, including spending a minimum of 20 minutes in a bath or shower. But at that point, I believed every single word the teacher told us, especially since that was said in perfect Russian, to ensure that we would have no problem understanding her.

That is why, despite my promise to Hashem, it took me a long time until I actually went to the *mikvah*. I wanted to go, but I held myself back until... until I felt I simply must take the plunge! I must keep my promise!

I remember that first time in the *mikvah* like it was yesterday. I assumed I'd find a dirty, decrepit building, full of germs and other horrible things. But I was determined to go, no matter what! After all, I had promised Hashem.

Entering the *mikvah* building, I made sure to hold my breath so that the stench wouldn't overpower me.

Instead, I found myself in a sparkling clean, well-illuminated reception room. The woman at the reception desk smiled at me. I couldn't understand what there was to smile about!

"I've come to immerse in the *mikvah*," I told her. I'm sure my face reflected my emotional state.

The woman stood up and told me to follow her. I was still afraid of what I'd find. She brought me into a sparkling clean, white tiled bathroom, which included a tall mirror, hangers, and a toilet.

Everything was so clean! I was absolutely flabbergasted!

"By the way, are you from Russia?" she asked me.

"Yes"

"Hmm… I guess you drew water from the well back there. Don't worry! I'll show you how to use a faucet. See the red handle? If you turn it this way, you'll have hot water, and the blue handle is for the cold water…"

I tried not to laugh.

The woman left and I took a long, relaxing bath. This bathroom was absolutely luxurious compared to the one in our rented apartment!

As soon as I completed my preparations, I pressed the button to call the *mikvah* lady. She was the same lady that I had met at the reception desk! She led me through a door to a large, shiny-white hall with many doors like the one I had just entered. In the middle of the hall was a small pool filled with clear, blue water.

I slowly descended the tiled stairs into the *mikvah*, and immersed in the water. The *mikvah* lady announced "Kosher!" I recited the blessing, reimmersed and returned to the same room that I had left.

I felt as if my soul was shining!

I almost danced home! At the time, I didn't understand why I felt so wonderful!

That was many years ago. Since that day, I have visited many *mikvaot*. Some are modest, some luxurious, but all are immaculate, and in all of them I experienced that glowing feeling of purity, something I will never give up for anything.

I recommend it highly.

୨୦

There are many myths and preconceived notions

that a 21st century woman must cast away before taking the plunge.

That is what this book will do for you.

It will reveal to you a world that is so wonderful and exciting, so powerful, that you will be swept away.

This world is exclusively ours.

It belongs to us, Jewish women.

This book lives up to its name.

It is ours, all of ours.

You are invited to join us on a journey to happiness.

So let's go, we are on our way.

The Power of Mikvah

John Gray Ph.D is a famous author and speaker who wrote the very popular book titled, *Men Are from Mars, Women Are from Venus*. Many years ago he delivered a lecture at Congregation B'nai Avraham in Brooklyn Heights on the topic of men and women. After the lecture, Rabbi Aaron Raskin, the Rebbe's emissary and Rabbi of this *shul*, asked Dr. Gray if he'd like to come take a look at their new *mikvah*.

When Dr. Gray saw the *mikvah* he said, "Wow! It's great, I LOVE the *mikvah*!"

The Rabbi asked, "What do you mean by 'I love'? Those are really strong words!"

Dr. Gray responded: "*Mikvah* is the greatest secret to a happy marriage."

"How do you know that?" Rabbi Raskin asked.

John Gray replied, "Well, to tell you the truth, when a couple comes to me and says, 'John, we're not getting along well together,' I instruct them to keep physically apart for just one week. I tell them to live in the same home, but to sleep in separate rooms and to be careful not to touch each other. During that time, they should focus on communicating verbally. I tell them to come back in one week and that then we'll discuss their problems. When the couple returns a week later they almost always say, 'John, we are so sorry! We were not able to stay apart for more than two-three days. We had to get back together. We hope you are still able to work with us!'

"'Well' I tell them, 'that was my objective, that you should come back together! Absence makes the heart grow fonder!'

"Therefore," continued Dr. Gray, "I really appreciate the concept of *mikvah*. It teaches us that a husband and wife should separate from time to time. As a result of that separation, when the woman immerses in a *mikvah* they join together again and are able to truly unite."

Dr. Gray's ideas are not original. "Absence makes the heart grow fonder" is a concept that has its roots in the Gemara. The Gemara (*Niddah* 3b) states, "A woman who is menstruating should separate from her husband, so that she will be beloved to her husband the same way that she was when she first entered the *chuppah* on the day of their marriage." Separation strengthens a couple's connection and passion.

Hashem commanded us to keep all of His *mitzvah*s. They connect us to Hashem. We keep the *mitzvah* of Family Purity because our Creator, blessed be He, told us to do so. Yet *mitzva* also have positive side effects and benefits.

One of the major positive benefits of keeping the laws of Family Purity is that it brings passion back into our marriage.

Rabbi Raskin once told a story about a lawyer from downtown Brooklyn. "He told me about his girlfriend in Florida. Every six months he visits her and together they have 'fireworks.' I said to him, 'I really feel bad for you. You have to wait for six months to get fireworks! In every Jewish home, each month there are fireworks. The night the wife comes back from *mikvah* is fireworks!"

***Mikvah* also brings Shalom Bayis**, domestic harmony, to a marriage. The word "Shalom," peace, suggests two separate entities that need to be united. To achieve that, the Torah prescribes times for embracing and times to refrain from embracing. This beautiful pattern of physical unity and separation

11

creates a unique dynamic, whereby time for physical contact alternates with creating a relationship based solely on a verbal and emotional connection. The Rebbe repeatedly stressed that closeness during the time when separation is necessary leads to unwanted separation at a time there is supposed to be closeness.

Another side benefit of *mikvah* is that it's a *segulah* to merit having healthy children. The physical welfare, emotional wellbeing, spirituality, and even livelihood of your future offspring is dependent on keeping the laws of Family Purity and having pure thoughts during intimacy.

And yes, we all have busy schedules. From morning until evening, the days, weeks, and years fly by. We barely have time to pause for a moment, to stop and take a breath. Although we often decide to make special time for ourselves, more often than not, we end up putting it on hold. But what if, no matter what, no excuses, you were obligated to spend an hour or so each month at a luxurious spa, an hour of pure relaxation solely for yourself? While the world is spinning around you at breathtaking speed, you'd calmly prepare yourself to become pure and renewed. Wouldn't you want that? Well, today, *mikvah*s are just as beautiful, clean and comfortable as the most luxurious spa!

And then, if you were to learn that going there would have a direct, long-lasting positive effect on your family and children, could you possibly say no?

***Mikvah* has a positive impact on our past.**

What can a woman do to correct having been negligent in going to the *mikvah* or not beeng aware of it's importance?

Some mothers wrote to the Lubavitcher Rebbe that their children had health, emotional,and other problems. The Rebbe often responded, "Find out if this child was born in purity, if his mother went to the *mikvah,* and if not, it's never too late. Though time marches forward, *teshuvah* works retroactively. In the physical world, it is impossible to turn the clock back, but *teshuvah* belongs to the spiritual sphere. G-d is infinite and the spiritual realm is above the constraints of time and space. Our *teshuvah,* our return to the faith of our Fathers, is in the spiritual realm. Therefore, *teshuvah* can correct spiritual damage that was incurred in the past. This is the strength of *teshuvah*!"

Mikvah is not only for young women in their childbearing years. A woman who no longer menstruates, due to menopause, a hysterectomy, or other reasons, must immerse in the *mikvah*, but usually only once. If you are married and your husband is Jewish, even if you have never gone to the *mikvah* before, you should immerse now. By doing so, not only will you continue to live in holiness and purity, but your immersion will have a retroactive impact on your past. In addition, going to the *mikvah* will have a positive impact on your children, grandchildren, and great grandchildren, for generations to come. A firm resolution to observe the laws of Family Purity from now on, as well as influencing others to do so, are suggestions for rectifying one's past negligence in keeping these laws.

Furthermore, it's never too late: if you haven't gone to the *mikvah*, go now, and inspire your children and friends to do so too! Try to persuade at least two or three Jewish friends who are married to Jewish men to start keeping the *mitzvah* of *Taharas Hamishpacha*.

If you are not married and therefore are unable to personally perform this *mitzvah*, you can help others. Increase charity. Give *tzedakah*, especially to institutions connected to *mikvah*. Help to renovate a *mikvah* or to construct a new one. You will be rewarded for each immersion that takes place as a result of your efforts.

It is better to give small amounts of *tzedakah* often, rather than a large amount at one time. The great Rambam said, that every coin that you dedicate for the *mitzvah* of *tzedakah* is counted as a separate *mitzvah*! This is why it's recommended to keep a special *tzedakah* box in your home, and to put some coins in it every day, except for Saturdays and Jewish Holidays, or even better, put money in the *tzedakah* box several times a day! Our Rebbe taught us to hang one *tzedakah* box on the wall. Why? This way the *tzedakah* box becomes an integral part of your home, transforming your home into a giant *tzedakah* box, attracting even more blessings. It's known that *tzedakah* sweetens judgment and brings the Redemption even closer.

&

"She certainly keeps the laws of family purity,

in which case G-d blesses her with healthy children,

with a long life and good years"

(Lubavitcher Rebbe, Igrot Kodesh, Vol.21, page 253)

I am Privileged

Ruchama's story:

I have the privilege of introducing women to the *mikvah*. Each time. I watch a woman's demeanor completely transform, I am awed anew. It is as if an outer layer is peeled away, enabling her inner radiance to shine forth. As one woman commented after taking the plunge, "I can't recognize myself. My face is literally shining!"

I am privileged! I have witnessed true miracles: babies born after years of infertility, singles finding their soulmates after years of searching, and seemingly unsolvable problems disappear.

So hello there! Let me introduce myself. My name is Ruchama and I am so pleased to meet you! I work in a hospital as a nurse, and have seven absolutely delicious grandchildren (and I am crazy over each of them). So as you can imagine, I am a very busy woman.

That's why, had you told me seven years ago that I would take a course to become a Family Purity counselor, I would have said that you have a wild imagination! But today, I teach brides about the *mitzvah* of *mikvah*, and give *shiurim* on *Taharas Hamishpacha* to married women, including many women who are learning about the beauty of *mikvah* for the first time. In addition, I arrange *chuppahs* and *farbrengens*. Two years ago, several friends and I got together to establish *Apirion*[1], an international

---

1   *Apirion,* a wedding canopy in Hebrew, is a non-profit organization dedicated to creating strong, Jewish families. They arrange for couples, mainly from the former Soviet Union, to sanctify their secular marriages with a kosher wedding.

organization that promotes *Taharas Hamishpacha* and encourages secularly married couples to have a *halachically* proper Jewish wedding.

When people hear that I established an organization, they often ask me why I did it, and what I personally get out of it. These are good questions. The answers are even better.

Eight years ago, when, between working full time and running my very busy household, I was so busy that I literally didn't have an extra minute for anything, a friend of mine begged me to go with her to a *shiur* on The Jewish Home. I immediately declined. After all, I was already observant and have always kept the laws of *Taharas Hamishpacha,* but my friend was persistent, and in the end, I went.

That lecture changed my life! The speaker, Rebbetzin Rachel Hendel from Tzfas, spoke about the *Kabbalistic* meaning inherent in the *mitzvah* of *Taharas Hamishpacha*. I was so moved by the power of what she was saying that I felt as if I was being aroused from a long winter hibernation.

The Rebbetzin explained that in the same way that Hashem gave each of us two eyes, two ears, two hands… He also gave each Jewish person two souls. According to Kabbalah, one soul is called the "animal soul," and the other soul is called the "G-dly soul."

The animal soul is responsible for our life force, our body's vitality. In addition, every Jew born to a Jewish mother has a G-dly soul, and sincere converts, who convert according to Halachah, Jewish law, merit to receive this G-dly soul upon ascending from their first immersion in the *mikvah*. The G-dly soul is the driving force behind our performance of Hashem's *mitzvah*s. This unique spark of divinity is a *Chelek Elokah Mima'al Mamosh*, "an actual part of Hashem Above."

They believe that through renewing and sanctifying one's marriage, they are inviting Hashem into their relationship and thus able to receive His long awaited blessings. Rabbi Aharon Shapiro, Rabbi of Pardes Katz, officiates at the *chuppahs* and supervises that everything is done according to Halachah. Their motto is: "Abba marries Ima".

Just as our bodies need clothes for protection, our souls require their own unique form of protection: "garments" uniquely tailored to fit each individual soul, "garments" that will protect these G-dly souls from harm. Via these "garments," Hashem channels His divine shefa (overflowing abundance) for our benefit.

I was fascinated by these ideas, but when the Rebbetzin said the following words, I could not possibly remain apathetic. She explained that during intimacy, at the moment of the greatest connection, Jewish parents have the power to influence the essence of their future child's "garment." When they unite in purity, through observing the *halachos* of *Taharas Hamishpacha* and having holy thoughts during intimacy, they bring down to their future child's soul a "garment" that is lofty and pure. When intimacy is consummated in holiness, this holiness, this *kedushah*, envelopes the woman and her future children.

I felt a new sense of meaning. Proper observance of the *mitzvah* of *Taharas Hamishpacha* determines the fate of our children! What a responsibility and what a privilege!

The Rebbetzin continued, "The *mitzvah* of *Taharas Hamishpacha* must be fulfilled exactly as prescribed, and not just 'more or less'." Then the Rebbetzin asked, "Is there any woman here who wants her children to be born 'more or less'?"

I was shaking. **I realized that my family's life and happiness, their very essence, depended on my keeping the *mitzvah* of *Taharas Hamishpacha* in an exacting manner.** But was I always really careful? Was the *mitzvah* always performed with perfection? But instead of crying over past mistakes, I came to the conclusion that I must look to the future.

I had a plan. It seemed simple, or so I thought.

What was my plan?

Step I: Self-examination, or *Cheshbon Hanefesh*. I realized that it was urgent that I take stock of the situation.

Step II: To ask the Rebbe, the leader of our generation, for a *brachah* immediately. It is my custom to ask the Lubavitcher Rebbe for his advice and blessings via his Igrot Kodesh, a collection of the Rebbe's correspondence. To do that, I first prepare myself to become a proper recipient of his blessings by giving *tzedakah* and taking upon myself a positive resolution. Then I write my question to the Rebbe on a slip of paper, and insert it randomly into one of the volumes of the Igrot. The Igrot is then opened at that place, and letters of both sides of the page are read. The response is amazingly accurate!

Step III: To ask Rebbetzin Hendel for direction on a practical level. I needed to know what I could do to correct the situation.

Dear Reader, I encourage you to also write to the Rebbe and ask him for a *brachah*. I'm sure that you have heard about the Lubavitcher Rebbe's work on behalf of Am *Yisrael*. He is the Nasi Hador, the Leader of our Generation, and he cares for every Jew, and he cares about you. Write to him, and you will see help and salvation.

A person must know how to ask, and even more importantly, know how to interpret the answer. Ask a Chabad Rabbi for assistance in both writing to the Rebbe and interpreting the answer correctly.

Through the Igrot Kodesh, the Rebbe blessed me with *hatzlachah* (success) for spreading the *mitzvah* of *Taharas Hamishpacha*.

I was flabbergasted. Me? Spread *Taharas Hamishpacha*? But Rebbetzin Hendel refused to let me take the easy way out.

While I was still trying to absorb the Rebbe's *brachah*, she influenced me so profoundly that today, eight years later, I cannot and will not stop. Instead, I look for the work and the work looks for me.

I feel as if the electrical current that aroused me then from my apathy, still does not give me any rest.

It's a pity to waste even one minute, for the sake of every woman. For the sake of every soul.

That is the answer to the first question, "Why did you decide to establish *Apirion*?"

And what do I get out of this? What do I gain?

It is impossible to put a monetary value on the *Hashgachah Pratis* and *Siyata DiShmaya* that I have had as a result of reaching out to teach the *mitzvah* of *Taharas Hamishpacha*.

How can you possibly place a monetary value on your sense of fulfillment when you see the face of a woman who has just immersed in the *mikvah* for the first time in her life? How can you set a price on a baby born after this immersion, especially when the woman has suffered twelve years of infertility?

I had the privilege of helping a lonely, single woman decide that one day she would observe the *mitzvah* of *Taharas Hamishpacha* and not long afterwards, with Hashem's help, she found her soulmate. I have helped an older couple sanctify their relationship through a kosher *chuppah*, according to Jewish law, and within the year their two sons, both over the age of thirty, found their brides.

I have been blessed to witness lives transformed. Blessed is He, and Blessed is His Name!

A close friend of mine once said, "Hashem gave us Jews a secret weapon called *Taharas Hamishpacha*. This *mitzvah* guards us and our children and grandchildren until the end of all generations."

So what have I gained from establishing *Apirion*? Through keeping these *halachos* and helping others to keep these *halachos*, we are drawing closer to our Creator. *Bonim anachnu LaHashem Elokeinu*, "We are sons of Hashem, our G-d," He guides us, watches over us, and saves us. When we move one small step closer to our Creator, He draws a hundred steps closer to us -- because we are His children.

A Purim Miracle

What do you say to someone that you haven't seen for a while? How are you? How are the kids? Perhaps you might compliment her on how she looks or on her beautiful necklace.

Ruchama, however, doesn't beat around the bush. "Nu, how is your daughter? Is she still going to the *mikvah*?"

A valuable question; a priceless answer.

Ruchama Rosenshtein was pleased with her friend, Genya's, response: "Yes, of course. Ina keeps everything, down to the very last detail!"

But Ruchama was not surprised. When one merits a miracle, one doesn't leave the source of the blessing so quickly.

Here's Ruchama's story:

A few years earlier, just before Chanukah, I learned that my friend Genya's daughter, Ina, was having fertility problems. She had undergone numerous treatments, and at her doctor's recommendation tried various therapies, but nothing seemed to help.

I knew of the best possible treatment!!

I invited Ina over to my house. After all, I knew of something that could help her, so how could I avoid my responsibility to help a Jew in need?

But Ina did not show up.

I wasn't one to give up, so I kept on phoning her again and again. I wasn't concerned that she might think I was pestering her. I simply wasn't about to give up. After all, it was for Ina's own good. Finally, I succeeded.

In very simple terms, I explained to this young, intelligent woman that having children can be compared to planting a seed in the earth. The first step is to prepare the ground. It must be ploughed and aerated. Then the seed is planted and carefully watered. If all these things are done, one can assume that the seeds will sprout and plants will grow. "To receive a blessing," I explained, "it is important to first prepare the foundations. Without that, there is no vessel to receive the blessing."

Ina listened, and she was convinced. Together, we decided to write to the Rebbe. After all, G-dly abundance is channeled to this world through the *Tzaddikim*.

Because Ina's problem was complex, she understood that she would need to prepare a large vessel, one capable of receiving a blessing. Although she was not yet Torah observant, she took it upon herself to keep the *mitzvah* of *Taharas Hamishpacha* in all its details.

The letter was written, folded, and placed in a volume of the Igrot Kodesh.

By *Hashgachah Pratis*, (Divine Providence), the page where we put the letter had many blessings on it. The one that caught my eye was mention of a "Purim miracle."

A miracle. That was exactly what Ina needed.

We parted ways, but not before I had put Ina in touch with a Russian-speaking *kallah* teacher that lived in her area.

One summer day, more than seven months later, I ran into Ina's mother. "How's everyone doing?" I asked. What I actually meant was "Any good news about Ina?"

Genya didn't keep me waiting. Her eyes literally sparkled as she blurted out, "My Ina is expecting…"

I was so excited. Yes, I see such miracles almost every day, but each time I'm moved anew.

I paused for a moment to think, and then asked: "Is she in her fifth?"

"How do you know?" Genya asked, completely perplexed. She waited for my response.

"The calculation is simple," I smiled.

Purim was exactly five months ago, and the Rebbe had clearly said: "A Purim miracle."

Tried and True Advice

Rita* is a woman in her fifties who was drawing close to Yiddishkeit. One day her husband started to suffer from extremely painful headaches. Tests pointed to something serious, probably a brain tumor. The question was, was it malignant or benign?

When Ruchama met Rita, she immediately understood that something was seriously bothering her. Ruchama is a nurse with plenty of experience in listening to people's problems, so it didn't take long for Rita to open up. She hoped that Ruchama could help her. After all, many people erroneously believe that medical professionals are privy to secret cures.

In this case, Rita was correct. Ruchama had a tried and true method to cure people's ills.

"Write to the Rebbe," she advised her.

"Well, I have nothing to lose," thought Rita, "and everything to gain."

Rita wrote to the Rebbe, doing everything according to the rules. First, she washed her hands and took upon herself a positive resolution. Then, she wrote the letter and inserted it into the Igrot Kodesh.

In his answer, the Rebbe wrote about the urgent need to take care of everything connected to the *mikvah*.

Mikvah? What's that?

This was the first time that Rita heard of it.

Ruchama assumed that it would not take extraordinary effort to convince Rita to accept G-d's blessing. After all, since women her age usually need to go to the *mikvah* once and then remain pure for the rest of their lives, there would be no drastic changes to her lifestyle.

But it was far from easy. Ruchama found it difficult to convince Rita to come to a Chassidic *farbrengen* even though she wouldn't have to do anything, so it was much more difficult to convince her to go to the *mikvah*! Eventually, however, Ruchama was successful. Rita realized that her husband's health was at stake. How could she not even give it a try?

Rita diligently studied the pertinent *halachos*. She counted the five days, then seven, and did all her preparations properly. When the big day arrived, she went to the *mikvah* accompanied by a friend.

Ruchama stayed in contact with her by phone. She was waiting to hear the good news. Finally, the moment arrived. In just a few minutes, Rita would immerse in the water and emerge as a new person, with a fresh, pure essence.

The *mikvah* lady waited. For her it was simply another woman going to the *mikvah*. For Rita, it was a momentous occasion.

The *mikvah* lady waited more, but Rita could not move. She was petrified, literally shaking with fear. She simply could not immerse in the water.

As it turned out, Rita suffered from hydrophobia, an irrational fear of water that had its roots in her childhood. It had been years since she had faced her fears. For close to fifty years she had avoided the beach and swimming pools, and as a result, she had forgotten about this bothersome phenomenon. Now, suddenly the phobia had reappeared. Rita was unable to enter the *mikvah*.

The *mikvah* lady was wonderful. With incredible warmth and patience, without a hint of blame or ridicule, she helped Rita overcome her fear and enter the water.

But although Rita could stand in the *mikvah*, she was incapable of putting her head under the water. The fear was greater than her. It overcame her. But for the immersion to be good, the entire head must be submerged in water, even if for only a split second.

They tried again and again. At one point, Rita was positive that for a split second she had managed to fully immerse, but the *mikvah* lady wasn't sure.

In the end, Rita had no choice but to emerge from the *mikvah* without completing the ritual immersion. She seemed not yet able to attain the *halachic* status of purity.

It was impossible to fathom, but there was no way to get around it. Rita got dressed in silence. She couldn't understand how such a thing could have happened to her.

 Rita's friend phoned Ruchama in frustration. It all seemed so senseless. "Why? Why? Why?" she shouted to Ruchama, "Write to the Rebbe. Now!"

Although Rita's friend was not yet religious, she knew exactly where to turn - to the Rebbe.

When Ruchama received the phone call, she was on her way home (from a Torah *shiur*, what else?). The moment she entered her house, she went straight to the shelf holding the Igrot Kodesh and without the usual preparations, she begged from the depths of her heart for a blessing for Rita. Then she opened at random the volume in her hands.

The answer was clear.

> *I enjoyed what was written about her visit… my hope is that finally her husband will also see the good and kindness of Hashem Yisbarach in this… (free translation, Igrot Kodesh Volume 22, page 337).*

Just as Ruchama finished reading these encouraging words, the phone rang. The *mikvah* lady was on the line.

"I just spoke to the Rabbi. He said that one of Rita's immersions was kosher."

"I know," Ruchama responded. "I already understood that from the answer I received from the Rebbe." Ruchama read the Rebbe's answer to the *mikvah* lady.

The *mikvah* lady was amazed. "You Lubavitchers know everything. From now on I'll call you whenever I have a problem."

Perhaps it's superfluous to mention that all of Rita's husband's medical problems disappeared. Baruch Hashem, he is completely healthy.

A Birthday Present

Was that the phone ringing?

Yup.

 Ruchama was fast asleep. She had just returned home from a long, exhausting night shift at the hospital. But the ringing continued.

It was Dr. Avraham Berliner*, a senior physician at the hospital.

Why was a senior doctor phoning a nurse at her private residence after she had just left a long, grueling night at the hospital?

"Dr. Rabinowitz* referred me to you," Dr. Berliner began. "He told me that you arranged a *chuppah* for him."

 Ruchama smiled at the memory. She and her friends at *Apirion* had arranged everything. It had been such an emotionally poignant evening. And now, it seemed that they were about to forge a new link in that eternal chain.

Dr. Berliner continued, "It's almost my wife's birthday. She asked for a very unusual present – a *chuppah*!"

Now Ruchama was wide awake. The adrenaline was rushing through her veins. She and her friends had lots of experience. They knew exactly what to do, which Rabbi to turn to, what to buy. Ruchama was already rushing ahead, arranging everything in her mind. Sleep? There's always tomorrow.

A few minutes later, Ruchama was on the phone with Dr. Berliner's wife, Chana*, also a senior doctor at the hospital. She was curious, and wanted to know exactly what she had to do to prepare for the *chuppah*.

Although Ruchama had prepared dozens of women for their *chuppah*, each time she explained what to do, she felt as though she was giving it over for the first time. But this time, she first wanted to understand something.

The Berliners had lived in Israel for many years. They were very well off, seemed happily married, and had wonderful children. So why did Dr. Chana suddenly desire a *chuppah*?

Ruchama was never one to be intimidated, so she asked – and Dr. Chana answered. This is her story:

Twenty years earlier, Dr. Chana had watched a television documentary about survivors of the Holocaust. One of the most emotional scenes was of Jewish couples standing under the *chuppah* as they set out to rebuild their lives according to Jewish Law. It was a scene that she could never forget. It symbolized Am *Yisrael's* rebirth after the Holocaust, and she knew, deep within her heart, that she, too, wanted it.

Now, twenty years later, she and her husband were fulfilling that dream.

Another Jewish marriage was sanctified. Another Jewish *chuppah*, and, once again, a husband and wife were joined together within the framework of their Jewish heritage that had so cruelly been taken away from them.

Another layer was peeled off. Another link was forged. One family, joined together by the holiness of Torah.

To outlive the "Straight Line"

Ruchama talks about one of her earliest students and the great treasure she received from her:

When I first started teaching *Taharas Hamishpacha*, I asked the Rebbe, leader of our generation, for his blessing for success in my work. The *brachah* that he gave me was immediately effective. It wasn't long before women started asking me to teach them. Marina*, a distant relative of mine, was one of the first to contact me.

The conversation with Marina started out like any typical phone call between relatives. She asked about my family, I asked about hers, and we shared interesting tidbits about the children. I assumed that she had called just to keep in touch. After all, family is family, and it's important to keep the channels of communication open.

But then, much to my surprise, she suddenly switched topics. "Ruchama, do you still go to Torah classes?" she asked.

I wasn't sure if she was serious or if she was just making fun of me, but I decided to give a straight answer. "Why yes, of course," I said.

"So tell me, what did you learn? What new resolutions did you take upon yourself?" she asked me.

I was flabbergasted!

"You know," Marina continued, "I was considering taking upon myself a *mitzvah* in honor of the New Year…"

I felt like dancing from excitement!

Hashem, Your People are so sweet! Marina seemed to be so far from being observant. I would have never dared to offer her to become more religious out of the blue!

Marina must have sensed my excitement because she quickly blurted out, "But I will never cover my hair. Ruchama, that's completely out of the question."

"Don't worry," I reassured her. "I won't ask you to cover your hair. I have a much simpler and easier *mitzvah* to suggest. What do you think about going to the *mikvah*?"

Today, Ruchama is used to speaking to people about the *mikvah*. But then, when she first started out, it was really hard. She wondered how she could ask a woman to make these kinds of changes in her life. And if the woman were to agree, how would she be able to tell her about all the intricate details involved in keeping this *mitzvah*?

I wondered if Marina would be willing to accept what I was about to tell her. She did.

Marina lives in the Galilee. I made inquiries to find the nicest *mikvah* in her area, arranged a *mikvah* appointment, and even found a Russian *mikvah* lady to supervise the immersion.

When I spoke to the *mikvah* lady about Marina, she blurted out, "This will improve her health." I was more than a bit taken aback. Although I have no doubt as to the truth of those words, I was surprised at how she had said them with such incredible confidence. So of course I asked her about it.

"Because of what happened in our family, I am positive that going to the *mikvah* will improve her health."

Ah, she had a personal story! And of course I always want to hear stories about this subject, which is so very close to my heart. But the *mikvah* lady was adamant. "This story is too personal. I don't tell it to anyone, and besides, no one would ever believe it!"

"So what?" I didn't understand. Shouldn't miracles be publicized, especially when it can convince others to keep the crucial *mitzvah* of *Taharas Hamishpacha*? I kept phoning her. I was insistent. I had to find a way to convince her to tell me. I tried again and again until finally, she agreed. I think that once you read her amazing story, you'll agree with me that my efforts were worthwhile.

Here is the *mikvah* lady's story:

My father had a serious heart problem. His heart was pumping at 15% the rate of a normal heart. His body was swollen. He was confined to a wheelchair and on oxygen twenty-four hours a day. It seemed as if every week some new complication sent him to intensive care, where the doctors had to work around the clock to save his life.

The situation was terrible. It seemed hopeless. I knew we had to do something. "Go to the *mikvah*," I told my mother again and again. But she didn't want to hear of it. She always had the same response, "Stop with this nonsense. It's just a bunch of old superstitions."

Then everything changed. My father was in intensive care. My mother and I were leaning on each other for support, staring at the heart monitor.

The line was flat.

My mother was shaking. "That's it!" she screamed. "I'm going to the *mikvah*." The moment she said these words, the line started to peak. My father's heartbeat had returned.

I had the merit of teaching my dear mother the laws of *Taharas Hamishpacha*. Although she was quite elderly, she merited to immerse in the *mikvah* that one time, and attain *taharah*. My beloved mother was privileged to correct her past and open the pipelines for future blessings.

It was astounding to see how quickly the *mitzvah* impacted my father's health. His doctors changed his medical regimen. Within days, he was healthy enough to return home. A month later he was a different person. He no longer needed oxygen, the swelling went down, and he even started to take walks outside. Most important of all, his mood improved dramatically and he was once again the happy and outgoing person who we all knew. He even wanted to play with the grandchildren. We couldn't remember the last time he had done that!

Basically, in the merit of my mother going to the *mikvah*, we got our father back!

I was amazed. When the *mikvah* lady finished her story, I couldn't help but ask, "Did you really want to keep such an incredible story to yourself? You must tell people! It's a *mitzvah* to publicize the miracle!"

Which is exactly what I'm doing here.

The Jewish Spark

Ruchama tells the following story:

This story is close to my heart. Whenever I remember it, I have a warm feeling that encourages me to continue my work with joy and strength. I merited seeing that with Hashem, and with the Rebbe, there is no distinction between a Jew who keeps *mitzvah*s and a Jew who does not. Every single Jew is precious.

Against all my expectations and without my having planned it, the Rebbe got me to leave Netanya and travel for over three hours, each way (!), to speak with an elderly Russian couple, both of whom were retired professors in their eighties.

Four days earlier I had received a phone call from my friend Dina. "Ruchama'le," she began. "You are the last person on my list. I've tried everyone, but I KNOW that you'll be able to help me. Let me explain. A few years ago we were introduced to an older Jewish couple, the Brandeins*. They had been prominent professors in Moscow, really special people. They left everything to come to Israel and help their daughter and their grandchildren.

"Their grandchildren became religious. Several years ago the grandchildren asked their grandparents, the Brandeins, to get married properly with a *chuppah*. The grandmother, Leah, promised to think it over, but so far, nothing's come of it. How long can this go on? So, Ruchama'le, I'm giving you my blessing that you have the privilege, *B'ezrat Hashem*, with G-d's help, of bringing this from the world of thought into the world of action!"

The Brandeins live in a small village about half an hour's drive from Jerusalem. It would take Dina and me some six hours just to travel there and back! I was more than willing to make the trip, but first I felt that I should ask the Rebbe. After all, perhaps there's a limit as to how much effort I should invest in this.

The Rebbe responded (free translation):

> *"The war of the Greeks was not against the wisdom of the Torah, but to make them forget 'Your Torah'. . .to take them away from the mitzvahs that are called 'Chukei Retzonecho' (statutes of Hashem's Will) and the children of Israel gave up their lives for these points, without making calculations with their own intellect etc. and they were successful with this conduct until it was laid down for everlasting generations and this for each and every one in Klal Yisrael to learn from. . .*
>
> *This letter was sent quickly and urgently. . .*
>
> *At an Eis Ratzon (an auspicious time) you will be remembered for the fulfillment of your heart's desires for good about all the issues you are writing about. . .with a blessing for good tidings in everything that has been said. . ."*

(Igrot Kodesh, Volume 23, page 70)

I let Dina know that I was up to this new adventure and that, with Hashem's help, we would be able to help this couple. I wondered how we would introduce ourselves. It's not like we could just show up from nowhere! But then I reminded myself that there was nothing to worry about. After all, we were following the Rebbe's directive! This was what he wanted from us.

Two hours after I had received the Rebbe's response, Dina called me with exciting news! Out of the blue, a relative of the Brandeins decided to broach the subject of *chuppah* with them, and as a beginning, she mentioned that somebody might come and talk to them. Now, the grandmother, the honorable professor Leah, was willing to allow two women to come to her house to discuss something with her. She had no idea what they wanted to talk about, but just the fact that she was willing to open her door and listen to two women that she had never met before was a huge step in the right direction.

A couple of days later Dina and I made the long journey from Netanya to Jerusalem and then spent an hour traveling on a bulletproof bus to a small village outside the city. I knocked on the Brandeins' door and a pretty, well-groomed woman opened it. She greeted us warmly. "There's no way that you're eighty years old!" I blurted out in surprise. Of course, after hearing such an obviously unrehearsed compliment, Madame Leah wanted to hear what else I had to say. But we didn't have much time. To catch the last bus from Jerusalem to Netanya we would have to leave in just three hours!

Madame Leah was a gracious hostess. She invited us into her living room. The table was covered with cookies and soft drinks, all with the most stringent standard of kashrus, and it had been purchased just for us. Her husband, the honorable Professor Brandein, was sitting on the armchair next to his wife. He apologized that he was hard of hearing, and proceeded to promptly fall asleep.

It's always a pleasure to converse with Russian intellectuals. There is so much to talk about – classical music, world literature, Mozart, Bach, Pushkin, Garcia! The conversation flows. It can continue for hours, which is exactly what happened here! The clock kept ticking, time was flying, we spoke for an hour and a half, and we still hadn't gotten to the point. The conversation continued; the Carmen Opera, Greek culture, and… nothing. We were no closer.

Dina'le tried her best to keep the conversation flowing. I used my secret ammunition; under my breath I whispered, "*Yechi Adoneinu Moreinu Verabeinu….*"

Suddenly, Madame Leah changed the subject and began to tell us about her granddaughter's adventures rafting down the rivers of South America.

This was it! Water! I had an opening! "Do you know that some women are so afraid of water that they refrain from using the *mikvah*?" I said.

Finally, I had said the magic word: *mikvah*! I quickly presented all the information, showed her the photo albums of Jewish weddings, and even presented Madame Leah with a pack of examination cloths.

Twelve minutes to go. The bus back to Jerusalem was leaving in another twelve minutes.

I concluded my presentation by telling her that there was no pressure, that she had free choice, and we'd contact her in a few days to find out what she decided to do. And then, hopefully, we could begin making arrangements for the actual *chuppah*.

"*Chuppah*?" asked the professor, who had been "sound asleep" in the armchair and was supposedly hard of hearing. "Our sixtieth anniversary is next week, so we'll celebrate it with a *chuppah*!"

"What? You've already decided?" The future *kallah* gave her groom a look that made me break out in a cold sweat. I tried to calm her down. "It's totally your decision," I said. "Only you can make this choice. No one can make it for you. There's absolutely no pressure whatsoever. You're in charge!"

"Okay, then call me back on Tuesday," she replied.

The bus was leaving in just five minutes. I had a volume of the Igrot Kodesh in my bag, so I suggested that the professor ask the Rebbe for his blessing.

"I never heard of your Rebbe!" he responded. "Who is he?"

Leah jumped up in anger. "What type of heresy is that? The Rebbe? This is THE Rebbe! Even I know that!"

 Two minutes to go. The professor opened the Igrot Kodesh and announced that he was requesting a blessing for his wife's health.

In the Rebbe's answer, the Rebbe gives his blessing for health and success in…Russian!

"Dear Baruch!

Your letter arrived late, and was only now received.

G-d will give the fulfillment of your wishes for good, and speedily, especially that now it is spring, when everything is being renewed and freed from the cold and freezing etc.

And so in good health and with a good mood, may you and all your family traverse these days, weeks and months. Wishing you happy Holidays, and everything that is good."

(Igrot Kodesh Volume 27, page 546)

We parted warmly and full of hope, Dina and I raced to the bus stop to catch our bus.

As promised, I phoned Mrs. Brandein on Tuesday.

Madame Leah answered the phone.

With a wry laugh she said: "It's okay. I've already started counting …"

She continued: "You should know that the only reason I am doing this is because you are so convinced that what you are doing is the right thing. I am going to the *mikvah* for YOU, so that YOU will have a *mitzvah*!"

I was so moved by her words! Hashem had sent us such a beautiful dear Jewish soul! I felt incredibly privileged to have merited meeting this wonderful Jewish woman who was prepared to do a favor for another Jew, even though she herself could not see the point in it! In her opinion, she was not gaining anything from going to the *mikvah*! I was experiencing a living Tanya *shiur*!

Leah decided to go to the *mikvah* in Jerusalem. Together with two friends, I met her at the central bus station and then we took her by taxi to one of the largest and most magnificent *mikvah*s in the city.

Leah was surprised to see that the *mikvah* is such a lovely, lively place: the telephone ringing off the hook, doors opening and closing, endless activity, and a waiting room full of women. Suddenly she realized that thousands of women keep this *mitzvah*. Baruch Hashem, she immersed properly, according to Halachah.

When she emerged from the *mikvah*, she still did not know what had pushed her to go through with it. With her wry laugh, she said: "Look at me! An old lady, eighty years old, who suddenly decides to go in the *mikvah*!"

"What do you think? I responded in jest. "Our father, Avraham, was circumcised at age ninety-nine, and afterwards three angels came to visit him. Now, here we are, me and my two friends, three angels who came to accompany you!"

Leah laughed. The entire way home she kept repeating, "My three angels… my own three angels!"

A few days later I phoned Leah and said, "Your three angels want to know when you will be having the *chuppah*."

"Fine," she responded. "Speak to my eldest grandson and he'll arrange everything. And I hope that my three angels will be there…"

They sang the Alter Rebbe's niggun at the *chuppah*. The eighty-something-year-old groom wore a white kittel, and his bride blessed everyone. The groom insisted on saying "*Harei at mekudeshet li*" in Loshon Kodesh. This was accomplished by writing out the words in large Russian letters.

Before the *chuppah*, I wrote to the Rebbe, and under the *chuppah*, the presiding Rabbi read the Rebbe's answer:

"Greetings and Blessing!

With pleasantness I received the good news that your sons and descendants plan to mark your fiftieth wedding anniversary in a fitting way. And surely, as with all such matters, this will be an opportune and fitting time to strengthen all matters of Torah and mitzvahs. May G-d add His blessings to them in good and holiness… together with all the members of the family and all participants.

Hashem Yisbarach will lengthen their days and years with goodness and pleasantness, and may the merit of their influence in being a living example, and words that come out of the heart, should encourage all the family members to go from strength to strength in all matters, including the main thing: real, chassidishe satisfaction from all their descendants …

With a blessing for a length of good days and years, and a kesivah vechasimah tovah l'shana tova umesukah, (a good writing and signing for a sweet new year) of both physical and spiritual matters."

(Igrot Kodesh volume 28, pages 304-305)

39

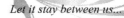

A Child's Cry

The Department of Religious Affairs sometimes refers brides who want to be taught in Russian to me, which is how I got to know young, sweet Sara.

The Rabbinate informed me that because of Sara's mother's medical condition, the family wanted to move the date of the wedding forward. At that point I had no idea of the complexity of the situation.

When Sara began to ask in depth about the *segulos* of going to the *mikvah*, and how this immersion could help another person, I tried to give her as much information as possible. At the end of the lesson, Sara told me decisively that she also wanted her mother to go to the *mikvah*. It would be her first time.

"Will she agree?"

"Yes." Sara was positive.

"Will she be able to do the internal examinations, the *bedikos*?" What would be after that? I didn't think that far.

"Yes, yes. Mother lights Shabbos candles, she says *Tehillim…*"

Sara was almost begging me to teach her mother.

Meanwhile, I learned that Sarah's mother had a serious lung condition and was on oxygen. "This is going to be complicated," I said to myself.

Although an older woman usually needs to go to the *mikvah* only once, for a woman who finds it difficult to breathe, even that one time might be too hard. So I decided that I'd first meet with her to decide if I would be able to take on the project. But it was Divine Providence that that never worked out. Something always happened at the last minute to prevent our getting together.

Looking back, I'm glad we never met. Had I seen her, I would never have wanted to take the risk, especially since I'm a nurse and understand all the medical ramifications.

But let's leave that for later.

Meanwhile the mother and daughter were waiting for my decision. How was I going to decide? That's right, you guessed it! I wrote to the Rebbe!

In a few words I described the complex situation. After all, that's all the Rebbe needs. In his response, the Rebbe brought down a story called "The Sound of a Crying Child"[1] about the Mittele Rebbe, and pointed out one of the practical applications of this story.

---

1 Prior to his becoming a Rebbe, Rabbi Dov Ber, the Mittele Rebbe (the 2nd in the chain of the Chabad dynasty), who was famous for his concentration skills, was once deeply immersed in learning Chassidus. Suddenly, in the same room, his youngest child fell out of a crib and began to cry. Rabbi Dov Ber was so engrossed in his learning that he did not hear the baby cry.

The Mitteler Rebbe's father, first Chabad Rebbe, Rabbi Shneur Zalman, who was learning on the top floor, came downstairs and calmed the child. Afterwards he asked his son why he had not taken care of his crying child. He responded: "I couldn't hear, I was deeply immersed in my learning".

The Alter Rebbe said: "When a Jewish child cries, you **must** to hear."

The following is a free translation:

"A person should be not so involved in any matter, even something very lofty, to such degree that he does not hear the sound of a crying child at his side, or near him…or even far away from him…he should help the child and do all in his capacity to give him whatever he is lacking.

This is especially true in our times, when there are many children and babies who 'fell out of their cribs' for whatever reason (or were not there to begin with) from the 'crib' of true Judaism, and they are crying out of distress of their souls. This soul is a chelek Eloka mimaal mamash, an actual part of G-d above, and is hungry and thirsty for the word of Hashem and His Torah and mitzvahs. No one is there to help them and to fulfill their lack in Chinuch Al Taharas Hakodesh, a pure, holy Education.

And so it is with many of our Jewish brethren, who, although old in years, are small, or babies in anything having to do with Torah, which is our life. It is forbidden to ignore the cries of these children of Israel…the instruction and the command and the order: Don't sin against the child! Stop doing anything you are doing and help the child, and return him to his father, Avinu Av Horachamon (Our merciful Father)."

(*Igrot Kodesh, Volume 22, pages 368-370*)

What can I say? There is no one like the Rebbe!
With Hashem's help I was able to teach the mother over the phone.

And then, again, in another display of *hashgachah pratis*, the mother and daughter would be going to the *mikvah* on the same night, right after the fast of Yud Zayin B'Tammuz (the 17th of Tammuz). Of course I was planning to be there, and a friend of mine, also a nurse, volunteered to be there as well. I made sure to inform the *mikvah* lady that this would not be a simple case.

My friend and I waited outside the entrance to the *mikvah*.

A cab stopped. Four women got out.

I recognized Sara, the *kallah*. She was supporting a woman who could barely walk. Her face was dark and her legs swollen. I heard her cough. From my work as a nurse, I knew that cough. I knew exactly what it meant. Oy Rebbe!!

My friend, who worked as a nurse in the I.C.U. was in shock. She whispered in my ear: "Stage 4!"

"Be quiet!" I warned her.

I wondered how the *mikvah* lady would react. Will she let her immerse?…

Nu, Hashem will help us. The Rebbe is with us!

My friend and I smiled at this brave woman. ""Hello, hello, everything is going to be just fine," I chirped, bluffing self-confidence. "*B'ezrat Hashem*. I'll immerse together with you." Although I was offering her words of encouragement, in truth, I was trying to encourage myself!

The woman was nervous, and rightly so. The tension only made her cough worse.

We slowly climbed the stairs. Whenever I am in a difficult situation, like this one, I repeat to myself "*Yechi Adoneinu…*".

"Hello, hello, please come in." the *mikvah* lady greeted us warmly. I gave a sigh of relief. Baruch Hashem! She was willing to help, despite the difficulties.

Sara, the *kallah*, went first. While she immersed in the *mikvah*, I remained with her mother in another room to help her with her final preparations. It wasn't easy. I pretended that I had complete self-confidence, but inside, I was quaking. We worked together, calmly and slowly. She had to stay calm, so that her breathing would remain steady....

Finally, the *mikvah* lady knocked to let us know that the *kallah* had completed her immersion and that now she would like to help her mother immerse.

Sara and her mother entered the *mikvah* together. It was an emotional and uplifting sight. The *mikvah* lady and I stood at the top of the pool, while the two women, mother and daughter, stood in the water. With Hashem's help, and despite the huge physical difficulties, they overcame all the obstacles and Sarah's mother was able to complete the *mitzvah* of purity.

It was a miracle that she succeeded in immersing three times in a row.

"Kosher! Kosher! Kosher!" the *mikvah* lady announced. It was a sight fit for the days of *Moshiach*. *Kamayim leyom mechasim*, (as the water covers over the sea, so G-dliness will be revealed at the time of the coming of *Moshiach*).

Back in the dressing room, the mother looked at herself in the mirror in astonishment. "Wow! My face has become light! Glowing! What is this? How did this happen?"

"You are holy and pure!." I responded with emotion. "It's the light of a *mitzvah*."

The *mikvah* lady also noticed the incredible change. "Amazing," she said. Your face is literally shining!"

The holy words of the Rebbe echoed in my ears:

"To everyone is directed the instruction, the command and the order: Don't sin against the child. Stop all of your other business and take care of the child. Return him to his Father, Avinu Av Horachamon, that he should learn his Father's Torah and do His mitzvahs and then he will live the meaningful, fruitful life, which is full, whole and good."

Chuppah in Afula, Israel. 85 year old kalla and 100 years old Chattan!

Holding a Tallis

Chana* is seventy-six years old. She is a wonderful, intelligent woman, and a proud grandmother of four. When she learned that an older woman who no longer gets her period needs to go to the *mikvah* once and then will remain pure for the rest of her life, she decided to take the plunge!

Chana was incredibly enthusiastic about preparing for this special experience. She followed the *Halachos* meticulously, counting five days and then the seven clean days (*Shiva Nekiyim*). Finally, she was ready to immerse in the *mikvah*.

Both her daughter and I accompanied her. How could I miss out on such a momentous occasion? What a merit to witness an older woman, a *Tinok SheNishbah*, who had never had the opportunity to learn about Yiddishkeit, immersing in the *mikvah* for the first and only time! Her heart was open to Hashem's Commandments and now, at the age of seventy-six, she was about draw purity and holiness to herself! Her family would also enjoy additional blessings as a result of their grandmother's bravery! What a great merit for an entire family!

Just as I was about to leave the house, it suddenly occurred to me that Chana might need assistance with the actual immersion. She had knee problems, and I was concerned that it might make it difficult for her to descend the stairs into the *mikvah*. Maybe she would need someone to enter the *mikvah* together with her?

I quickly grabbed my bathing suit before racing out of the house. It's a good thing I did; Hashem was watching over me.

Chana had been so involved in getting ready go to the *mikvah* that she completely forgot that the actual immersion might be problematic! It could be that since she had never actually visited a *mikvah*, she had no idea what it involved. But the moment she saw the steps going down into the water, she stood in shock and said, "I can't. I can't go down those stairs. They're too steep. My knees don't bend."

Thank G-d, I had come prepared!

"Chana, just one sec'," I said with full confidence. "I'll change into my swimsuit and go down with you. I'm a nurse, so I have lots of experience in helping people with physical challenges. I am absolutely positive that you'll manage just fine! Don't worry, you'll manage to immerse in the *mikvah*!"

A few moments later, I found myself in the *mikvah* – again, after so many years! Chana stood there, still taken aback at my confidence and firmness. And then, almost without her realizing it, she had descended the steps and was surrounded by the waters of the *mikvah*.

Chana was still trembling slightly. "There's nothing to be afraid of!" I reassured her. "You've gone this far, so, with Hashem's help, you'll go even further. Don't worry. I'll hold you on both sides, and will only let go for a second."

Although she was afraid, Chana really wanted the merit of immersing in the *mikvah*. She tried to cooperate, but it was difficult. After all, she was seventy-six years old and had physical limitations. She tried to bend down, but she couldn't. No matter how hard she tried, she was incapable of putting her head under the water.

Suddenly, I remembered something that a *mikvah* lady had once taught me. I lightly tapped Chana's head, and suddenly, she bent down low enough to immerse properly. Chana immersed three times in the *mikvah's* waters! We were so excited. For the first time in her life, Chana was a *T'horah*! And she would remain that way for the rest of her life!

Upon returning home, I wrote to the Rebbe about this uplifting experience. Here is his response (free translation):

The commentary of Toras Hachassidus on the Mishna, 'Two holding a Tallis, this one says I found it, the other says I found it', etc. is well known. The inner meaning learned from this is that anyone who helps his friend, whether he be big or small, in a matter of Torah and mitzvahs, acquires a part of that mitzvah and can demand: 'I found it.' Moreover, our Sages of blessed memory state that 'The one who causes the action is greater than the one who does the action.'

(Igrot Kodesh, vol. 28, page 263)

No commentary necessary.

A Happy Mother of Children

A friend's tale:

Dudi* stood at his wife, Yonit's, bed, searching for a flicker of awareness in her unseeing eyes. The monotonous beeping of the ICU machines seemed to be mocking him: That's it…it's finished…it's over…chas v'shalom! He shook himself. This can't be happening… again! His shoulders heaved and he broke down in tears.

He had begun his second marriage only three years earlier. Before that, he had been happily married to Chagit*. Together, they had made the journey to Yiddishkeit, learning Torah and keeping the *mitzvah*s. Then, once all their children were married, Chagit passed away after a long and difficult illness.

Dudi married Yonit when he was already a grandfather. Yonit had come to know her Creator at the age of forty. The "young" couple had two children together. Their house was full of life and joy and Dudi felt like a young man again!

Then, in the middle of Yonit's eighth month of pregnancy, she suddenly had difficulty breathing. She was rushed to the hospital. Her organs started to fail and she was then attached to a respirator, in an induced coma, and her condition seemed to be getting worse by the minute. None of the doctors understood why this was happening to her or what they could do to help her.

Yonit gave birth to a beautiful, healthy baby girl with an emergency C-section. The joy of the baby's first cry was marred by the knowledge that she might never merit to know her mother.

Many prayers were said and many tears were shed as people pleaded with Hashem that Yonit recover to fulfill her dream, together with her husband, of raising a beautiful Torah family.

Devorah, a relative, felt she had to do something exceptional for Yonit's merit.

She had recently heard about a woman who experienced a medical miracle after donating money to renovate a local *mikvah*. Devorah made a contribution to the local *mikvah*. The treasurer of the women's committee in charge of renovating the *mikvah* wrote to the Rebbe, asking him for his holy blessing for Yonit's recovery.

With a pounding heart she placed the letter into a volume of the Igrot Kodesh. When she opened the Igrot Kodesh, she was surprised to see that it had opened to a letter from the Rebbe thanking a woman for her donation to the *mikvah*…!

When Devorah heard about the Rebbe's response, she doubled the amount of her original donation, and then waited anxiously to see the Rebbe's *brachah* materialize.

Four days passed. Yonit began to show signs of recovery. Every day there was a change for the better. Despite all the dire forecasts, Yonit started to breathe on her own.

And then she opened her eyes.

When Yonit finally hugged her newborn daughter for the first time, the entire medical team was there to see the miracle

There was not a dry eye.

Hashem Does Not Remain In Debt

Ruchama's story:

Have you ever felt a sudden almost overwhelming urge to pray for no apparent reason? Did you ever open up a Sefer *Tehillim* and start to say the words, without understanding why?

This happens to many people. It's not rare. In some cases, an hour later, or perhaps a day later, the reason becomes clear. Prayer always helps. Sometimes, we see that clearly and at other times, well, we just know that it does.

I have been asked more than once what "I get out of" my intensive work in spreading the *mitzvah* of Family Purity. I feel that it's impossible for me to finish my collection of stories without telling one that demonstrates that Hashem really does repay His debt.

That's the way it is. When a person does *mitzvah*s with joy and *mesirus nefesh*, refuses to let obstacles get in the way of doing what needs to be done to bring purity and holiness to this world, and causes others to bring purity and holiness into this world, Hashem repays him, sometimes with outright miracles.

Baruch Hashem, on many different occasions I have had the privilege of seeing this in my own life.

My daughter, Leah Malka, is my right hand (wo)man in the organization. When we arrange weddings for older couples from Russia *k'daas Moshe* v'*Yisrael* (according to the Law of Moshe and Israel) she takes a day off of work to attend the ceremony, sometimes traveling an hour and a half each way. She prepares everything, sets the tables, serves the food, and even takes photographs (she's a great photographer. I'm not at all prejudiced, even though she is my daughter …)

The story I want to tell, happened on a Saturday night, *motzei Shabbos* Hagodol, the Motzaei *Shabbos* before Pesach.

There had been two weddings arranged for that same week - and this final week before Pesach is always the busiest week of the year, even without having to organize weddings! Leah Malka worked tirelessly to make sure that everything was perfect, and it was! The people who had been involved in arranging the weddings were exhausted, which is why I made sure that my daughter and her husband would come to spend Shabbos with us. They both needed the rest!

Motzei Shabbos, they left to return to their home in Kiryat Malachi, and I went to work on the night shift at the hospital. Suddenly at half past three in the morning, I got a text message: "Mother are you asleep?"

I wasn't, but why was Leah Malka awake at this hour?!

I phoned her immediately. Her voice was shaking: "Don't worry, everything's fine. There was a fire in our house."

Let's backtrack to two and a half hours earlier. Somewhere between one and two in the morning, I had an unexpected break in my work. And so, seemingly without any good reason, I decided to use this free time to say *Tehillim*. Yes, in the middle of the night, without knowing what was happening to my daughter, I recited *Tehillim*.

I, the mother who had brought her into this world, sat in Netanya, a two-hour journey from Kiryat

Malachi, and recited *Tehillim*, chapter after chapter.

Meanwhile, this is what happened in Kiryat Malachi:

The owner of my daughter and son-in-law's rented apartment lives in the apartment directly over theirs. She arrived home very late that night and smelled something burning. She checked her entire apartment and found nothing suspicious.

Then she went downstairs to check my daughter's apartment. She peered through the kitchen window and saw that the table was in flames!

She rang the bell, but my daughter and her husband were so soundly asleep that they did not wake up. The telephone was on the kitchen table, so phoning wasn't an option.

The hall from the kitchen to the bedroom was about 16 feet long. The bedroom door was shut, but the hallway was full of smoke and soot. Meanwhile, my daughter and son-in-law were blissfully asleep, with no idea that anything was amiss!

The landlord phoned the fire department. They broke into the kitchen and extinguished the fire.

Meanwhile, the young couple continued sleeping! They finally woke up when a fireman knocked on their bedroom window.

The hallway and living room were full of thick smoke and soot. There was no electricity of course, everything was dark. It was hard to breathe.

They felt their way to the front door, and, with Hashem's help, they managed to get out.

Once they got over their initial shock and began to process what had just happened, they realized that they had experienced a great miracle.

First of all, they had left the key in the lock of the front door. If they had not done so, how, when they were panicking in the dark, would they have found it to be able to open the door? Just outside their apartment were two huge gas canisters, right next to the wall where the fire had first broken out. Thank G-d they did not catch fire and explode! We can't imagine what would have happened if they had!

But this is not everything.

Only the plastic table was destroyed. Although the washing machine, refrigerator and oven were covered with soot, they were undamaged.

The most incredible thing, which my daughter told me then, at three thirty in the morning, was that everything that had been on the table was completely destroyed, except for a *sefer* about the Laws of the Holidays. It was only partially burnt. The fire had stopped at the Holiday of Pesach, the Holiday we were about to celebrate that very week!

My daughter was shaken, and overwhelmed with emotion.

I had something to add to this wondrous list of miracles. At exactly the same time when all of this was going on, while my daughter and her husband were sound asleep as the fire raged, our Father in Heaven arranged my work schedule. He provided me with a window of opportunity and I took advantage of it in the best possible way. I said *Tehillim*.

"When did this all happen?" I asked Leah.

"Between one and two in the morning," she replied.

"Yes, of course." A full circle. Thank you Hashem!

I wrote to the Rebbe with great emotion about the miracle (miracles!) that had happened to us.

Here is the Rebbe's response (free translation):

> *"You have merited and are there in Eretz Yisrael, the land that the eyes of Hashem Elokeinu are on, from the year's beginning to the year's ending.*
>
> *He will not slumber and will not sleep, the guardian of Israel...*
>
> *...With Blessings for Good Tidings."*

You tell me, would not one more word be superfluous?

Four Chuppot in one day at Brodsky Synagogue, Kiev, Ukraine

Exerpt from the Rebbe's Letter

Mrs.____

Albany, N.Y.

Blessing and Greeting:

I am in receipt of your letter of May 21st, in which you write about your background and some highlights of your life.

In reply, I will address myself at once to the essential point in your letter, namely your attitude towards religious observance, as you describe in your letter, and especially to the particular *Mitzvah* which is most essential for happy married life, namely *Taharas Hamishpacha*. You write that you do not understand the importance of this *Mitzvah*, etc. This is not surprising, as is clear from the analogy of a small child being unable to understand a professor who is advanced in knowledge. Bear in mind, that the condition between the small child and the advanced professor is only a difference in degree and not in kind, inasmuch as the child may, in due course, not only attain the same level of the professor, but even surpass him.

It is quite otherwise in the difference between a created being, be he the wisest person on earth, and the creator Himself. How can we, humans, expect to understand the infinite wisdom of the Creator? It is only because of G-d's great kindness that he has revealed certain reasons with regard to certain *Mitzvos*, that we can get some sort of a glimpse or insight into them. It is quite clear that G-d has given us the various commandments for our own sake and not in order to benefit Him. It is therefore clear what the sensible attitude towards the *Mitzvos* should be. If this is so with regard to any *Mitzvah*, how much more so, with regard to the said *Mitzvah* of *Taharas Hamishpacha*, which has a direct bearng not only on the mutual happiness of the husband and wife, but also on the wellbeing and happiness of their offspring, their children and children's children.

It is equally clear that parents are always anxious to do everything possible for their children, even if there is only a very small chance that their efforts would materialize, and even if these efforts entail considerable difficulties. How much more so in this case, where the benefit to be derived is very great and lasting, while the sacrifice is negligible by comparison. Even where the difficulties are not entirely imaginary, it is certain that they become less and less with actual observance of the *Mitzvah*, so that they eventually disappear altogether.

Needless to say I am aware of the "argument" that there are many non-observant married couples, yet they're seemingly happy, etc. The answer is simple. First of all, is it well known that G-d is very merciful and patient, and waits for the erring sinner to return to him in sincere repentance. Secondly, appearances are deceptive, and one can never know what the true facts are about somebody else's life, especially as certain things relating to children and other personal matters are, for obvious reasons, kept in strict confidence.

As a matter of fact, in regard to the observance of *Taharas Hamishpacha*, even the plain statistics of reports and tables by specialists, doctors and sociologists etc., who cannot be considered partial towards the religious Jew, clearly show the benefits which accrued to those Jewish circles which observed *Taharas Hamishpacha*. These statistics have also been published in various publications, but it is not my intention to dwell on this at length in this letter.

My intention in writing all the above is, of course, not to admonish or preach, but in the hope that upon receipt of my letter you will consider the matter more deeply, and will at once begin to observe the *Mitzvah* of *Taharas Hamishpacha*, within the framework of the general Jewish way of life which our Creator has clearly given to us in His *Torah*, which is called *Toras Chaim*, the Law of Life. Even if it seems to you that you have some difficulties to overcome, you may be certain that you will overcome them, and that the difficulties will be only in the initial stages.

I understand, that in your community there are young couples who are observant and you could discuss this matter with them, and find out all the laws and regulations of *Taharas Hamishpacha*. If, however, you find it inconvenient to seek the knowledge from friends, there are booklets which have been published, which contain the desired information, also a list of places where a *Mikvah* is available. . .

The Power of One Grandmother

As heard from Rabbi Aaron Raskin.

(in memory of my grandmother, Gittel bat Koppel ז״ל)

Esther's grandparents immigrated to the United States from Germany in 1905 and settled in North Dakota. When they arrived, they were strictly Torah observant, but as they integrated into the community, their adherence to Torah slowly weakened. Their four daughters distanced themselves even further from Torah observance. One of them, Beatrice, became completely secular.

Beatrice eventually married a Jew, thank G-d, and the young couple moved to Minnesota where their daughter, Esther, was born. When Esther grew up, she became attracted to Judaism. It was as if she was being pulled by a magnet.

Esther became religious through Chabad. She attended Bais Chana Seminary, and was soon fully *mitzvah* observant. She married a young Lubavitcher chassid, and together the new couple dreamed of building a big happy family with cheerful, healthy kids. But time passed quickly and their dream did not materialize. There were no children.

Esther did everything humanly possible. She was careful with all the *mitzvah*s, and of course she regularly went to the *mikvah*, stringently observing all the details of *Taharas Hamishpacha*. She even frequented classes on *Taharas Hamishpacha* to be 100% positive that she doing everything right.

At the same time she also started medical treatments, yet the long-awaited pregnancy did not occur. In moment of despair Esther wrote a letter to the Lubavitcher Rebbe. Writing like a daughter to her father, she poured out her heart and described all her pain and difficulties.

Two days later, Esther received a phone call from New York. It was Rabbi Groner, the Rebbe's secretary. He told her the Rebbe's request: "Ask your mother to immerse in the *mikvah*."

Beatrice's reaction was strong. She was puzzled and irritated. "What's the connection between my plunging into the *mikvah* and you having a baby?!" she asked sarcastically. "What are these religious prejudices in an era of technological progress?! No way!"

Esther wrote to the Rebbe again, this time about her mother's refusal to go to the *mikvah*.

Rabbi Groner called her back. The Rebbe advised Esther to persuade her grandmother to go to the *mikvah*! Grandma Jenny was still alive, as was Esther's grandfather, Levi Yitzchak!

Ester begged her grandmother, "I want to give birth to your great-grandchildren! I did everything possible to have a baby: I went to doctors, I carefully observe *Taharas Hamishpacha*, but nothing helped. The Lubavitcher Rebbe promised that I'll have a baby if you agree to go to the *mikvah*! Can you please help me?"

Grandma Jenny was hesitant. She asked her husband, Grandpa Levi Yitzchak, what he thought. Should she agree?

"What would grandparents not do for the sake of their grandchildren?" Levi Yitzchak smiled to his wife. "Of course you should go to the *mikvah*."

So sweet, soft-hearted Grandma Jenny went to the *mikvah*. As she immersed in the pure, clean water, she recalled her first time in a *mikvah* as a bride. She regretted the many years that she was able to keep this *mitzvah*, but did not, and was grateful that she finally merited immersing in purity.

Esther conceived one month later.

Today, she has nine beautiful children.

૭૩

The Rebbe, the leader of our generation, taught:

just as the generation of Egypt was redeemed in the merit of righteous Jewish women,

our generation, too, will be redeemed

in the merit of righteous Jewish women.

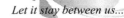

A House Check

Ronit* tells her story…

I moved to Israel with my husband and three adorable girls from the Caucasus, located between the Black and Caspian Seas. At the time, I considered three children a large family. In Israel, I gave birth to our fourth daughter, so then we became a <u>huge</u> family!

On my own I slowly learned about the *mitzvah* of *Taharas Hamishpacha*. I read many books and asked lots of questions. I really liked the idea of observing this *mitzvah*. I understood the logic behind it and started keeping it.

Shortly after I started using the *mikvah*, I became pregnant. Yes, I was pregnant, but, much to my sorrow, I did not merit a child. For nine months, I held that precious child in my womb, but I never merited holding him in my arms. It was very difficult for me to get over this painful episode, and someone suggested that I write to the Rebbe, telling him how I was feeling.

I accepted the advice, and placed my letter in the Igrot Kodesh. The page we opened contained instructions to check our *mezuzos* and *tefillin*, and to learn how to perform the *mitzvah* of *Taharas Hamishpacha*. We immediately followed the first instructions. My husband sent the *mezuzos* and his *tefillin* to a qualified *sofer* to be checked. But what about the second instructions? I had no idea how I should relate to that. After all, I had been observing this *mitzvah* for some time already, and it didn't seem as though the Rebbe's instructions applied to me.

Another pregnancy that ended without a baby brought me again to the Rebbe. This time, my frustration was even greater. One time could be a coincidence, but twice? Without any medical reason?

In the answer I received from the Igrot Kodesh, I received a blessing for a son, but again the Rebbe wrote about the importance of learning the *halachos* of *Taharas Hamishpacha* and the laws of immersing in the *mikvah*.

I understood that I needed to look deeper. I turned to a Rebbetzin and asked her to review the *halachos* with me. One of the first questions she asked me was, "How do you do the *bedikos*?"

"*Bedikos*???" I looked at her without understanding. "What are *bedikos*?"

I knew that I had to separate, to count seven clean days, and to go to the *mikvah*. But I had never heard about the *bedikah* of *hefsek taharah* or that I was supposed to perform two *bedikos* a day!!!

I had learned on my own!

Simply put, my *tevilla* (immersion in the *mikvah*) had been worthless.

Do you understand what that means? I thought I was keeping the *mitzvah*, but in reality, I was not.

But the Rebbe knew.

I began again, this time properly. I was careful about every detail. I was truly keeping the laws of *Taharah*.

The next pregnancy progressed normally.

When I went into labor, I wrote to the Rebbe and asked for his blessings for an easy, normal birth and that I deliver a healthy, normal baby.

I delivered a healthy, sweet baby. We named him Menachem Mendel, after the Rebbe. Obviously.

After that, we had another four children. Three boys and a girl, all healthy. Nine children. We felt blessed.

But the blessing continued. When I was forty-four (!), and my three oldest daughters were already married, I merited another rare and precious gift: another daughter, our youngest!

A complete minyan, ten children, *Bli Ayin Hara.*

&

"It is not as popular opinion often claims that children burden one's life and cause problems. In fact, the opposite is true. There is no greater disorder, nor such a vast amount of troubles in any home (also among non-Jews) than is caused by mixing into the patterns of life, as in the example of the so-called "family planning". This are generally known and publicized facts."

(adapted from Rebbe's speech from 1980)

A Miracle within a Miracle

Miriam* was the mother of three wonderful children. Her life was completely normal and peaceful, until suddenly everything changed. She developed a serious blood disorder. The treatment was extremely uncomfortable: painful injections of blood thinner into her stomach twice a day. After two weeks, there was no place left on her stomach for the injections. Physically, it was torture. After a month and a half, things became easier. The shots were replaced with lifelong treatment pills and regular blood tests.

Miriam started to get used to her condition. "You're not allowed to become pregnant in the near future," the doctors told her. "And when you do, you'll have to have the shots twice a day for the whole nine months, as well as for an entire month prior to conception (!)."

Miriam shivered at the thought of the painful injections.

At the end of the critical first year, when life was beginning to return to normal, Miriam's husband surprised her by saying: "Three children are not enough. I really want more."

That one sentence threw Miriam into a dilemma. She also wanted more children, but how could she cope with ten months of painful injections? She couldn't even think of it.

She wrote a letter to the Rebbe and placed it in the Igrot Kodesh. The page she opened contained two letters. In the first, the Rebbe wrote: "Mazal Tov on the birth of a girl." How encouraging! The second letter was even more surprising. It was a *brachah* for a *Refuah Shleimah* and the hope that in the near future she would not need any more medicine.

That was much more than Miriam had hoped for! A blessing for pregnancy- yes! But it was hard to believe that with her diagnosis she would ever be off "lifelong" blood tests and medication.

Miriam courageously decided to have another child. Every day, she had two injections into her stomach. It was far from simple, but the Rebbe's letter gave her the inner strength and courage to continue.

But in addition to the pain of the injections, the shots had an unwanted side effect. Miriam was having difficulty reaching the point where she could actually go to the *mikvah*, and if she went to the *mikvah* late, chances were that she would not get pregnant and all the shots would have been for nothing!

Miriam wrote a second letter to the Rebbe. He advised her to go to a different expert.

During this time, Miriam participated in the Nshei Chabad Women's convention. And, as if it had been arranged especially for her, the main theme of the convention was "Encouraging Childbirth."

No more and no less.

At the convention, a very moving letter from the Rebbe was read out loud. Miriam listened intently.

The Rebbe requested that women should not be afraid to have more children and promised that their health would be strengthened!

And if Miriam needed any additional encouragement, one of the women there allowed her to hold a dollar bill from the Rebbe.

Miriam was super-excited.

During the break between sessions, Miriam phoned to make an appointment at the clinic of a well-known professor. Perhaps he would be the right person to help her.

The day of the appointment arrived. Of course, Miriam came to the meeting with all her medical documents. But, she also came with faith in the Rebbe's *brachah*. Already, during the first minutes of the appointment, this faith proved itself.

The professor said unequivocally that that the obstetrician she had been using had been overly cautious. One injection per day was sufficient – half the suffering, Baruch Hashem.

Miriam followed the professor's instructions and started taking the daily injection prior to conception. But when she was finally able to go to the *mikvah*, it was three days before she was scheduled to start her next cycle. According to nature, the chances of conceiving were almost nil.

But Miriam wasn't upset. She had the Rebbe's *brachah*.

When Miriam arrived at the *mikvah*, six women were ahead of her, waiting in the lobby. Although she was shy and was never one to speak in public, she was still under the influence of her visit to the "Holy Courts" of Lubavitch headquarters at 770 Eastern Parkway, New York.

How could a group of women sit quietly without hearing some words of Torah? Somehow, from an unknown inner space, Miriam found the courage to speak up and read a short Dvar Torah from the Sichos Hashavuah weekly paper that was on the coffee table. She felt that her future depended on it.

Much to Miriam's surprise, the women there were enthusiastic about the spontaneous *shiur*. A lively discussion took place and the atmosphere in the waiting room became warm and friendly. Miriam was ecstatic. She had overcome her natural inclination and conquered her inner fear.

Later, standing in the *mikvah*, Miriam took her time to ask Hashem to fulfill the prayer of her heart, to bestow on her a healthy child.

She went home, glowing. Miriam felt, she knew for sure: that this night would be THE night.

The following day, Miriam was sitting at her office desk, immersed in her work. Suddenly she dropped her pen as she felt as if a gentle wave had passed through her body. She had never felt this way before. She smiled quietly to herself. She had not the slightest doubt that she had conceived.

Just a few days later, a test confirmed that she was pregnant.

"You understand that there is no medical explanation for this, don't you?" The doctor wanted to be sure she got the point.

"A medical explanation? Who needs it?" she retorted. "I have the Rebbe's blessing, and that's enough."

But this is not the end of the story. It's just the beginning.

In one of the many letters that Miriam wrote to the Rebbe during this miraculous pregnancy, she received a response concerning an invasive examination.

Miriam did not share the contents of the letter.

Months went by. The due date came and went.

When Miriam arrived at the hospital with contractions, the doctors saw that she needed intravenous medicine to induce stronger labor. They asked Miriam if she would like them to induce the labor immediately or wait until the following day.

Miriam said that she wanted time to think. The truth, however, was slightly different. Miriam needed this extra time in order to write to the Rebbe.

This time, unlike like previous times, there was no clear answer.

The letter spoke about children's education, (Chinuch), birth was not mentioned. But the date at the top of the letter said it all: 24th Nissan.

That day's date was 22[nd]Nissan. Miriam understood that the baby would be born in another two days, on 24th Nissan.

She asked to be discharged and the doctors agreed.

The next day, towards evening, Miriam returned to the hospital. She was examined, but there was still no change. "I don't want to be induced," she said. "Give me an hour or two."

"Do you want to go home again?" the doctor asked, half joking.

"Not at all," was Miriam's definite answer.

It was already the eve of 24th Nissan. Miriam had no doubt that she would give birth that day.

An hour and a half later, it became clear that Miriam was not leaving the hospital. The baby was in distress and she was taken for an emergency caesarean section.

At the time of the surgery, it became clear that inducing the labor would have endangered the baby's life.

A beautiful, healthy baby boy was born on 24th Nissan. Everyone was happy, except perhaps for Miriam's oldest daughter, who had prayed for a younger sister.

After the birth, when Miriam went to see the professor again, he told her that she no longer needed "lifelong" treatment!

And yes, her oldest daughter's prayers were not in vain - afterwards she went on to have three more younger sisters!

ॐ

"G-d gave everyone, and the Jewish women in particular (as the foundation of her home) all the necessary ability and talents to guide her household and influence Jewish women around her. She can encourage them to follow this path, which does not "mix up" G-d's prescribed order, and to adherently observe the laws of Family Purity, which guides the relations between husband and wife in the best possible way."

(adapted from Rebbe's speech from 1980)

Like a Bride on the Day of her Chuppah

It would take an entire book to record all of the obstacles that Raya had to overcome before she merited to immerse in the *mikvah*. So how can I tell over an entire life's story in a few pages? But still, something has to be written so that when you, the Jewish woman reading these lines, think that something is difficult or impossible, you'll remember Raya and your perspective will change.

Raya moved to Israel when she was fifty years old, an accomplished woman, with half a century of living behind her.

At the age of fifty Raya discovered her Jewish heritage. She grabbed the treasure with both hands and started keeping *mitzvah*s.

It's easy to write about her challenges, but it was not easy for her to face them. Fifty is far from young, and changing habits is never easy, even for someone in their twenties.

Raya bravely turned her entire life around. But the biggest obstacle to full Torah observance was her marriage. Her husband wasn't Jewish. Through the years they convinced themselves that their marriage is "happy" since from materialistic perspective their lives was settled down, at least they hadn't any complaints on each other... Why should they change it? Why to go through all the pain?

At first, Raya's husband was willing to look into Judaism. He even considered converting. What a wonderful solution, they thought! They would remain happily married, and even celebrate a *chuppah* after almost thirty years of marriage. After all, everyone knew that Ruchama would make all the arrangements!

Everything seemed so perfect! What a happy ending! But then, at the last moment, Raya's husband changed his mind. He decided that Judaism was not for him. And they both decided that their marriage have no future.

> *"It is revealed and known to everyone, even to non-Jews, that the existence, power and inner strength of the people of Israel stem from the forefathers and mothers of this people and are the inheritance of each and every one of the sons and daughters of the Jewish people. It is a natural part of our souls, at all times and places. This is what it makes us into a very special people within this world: "Lo, it is a people that shall dwell alone and among the nations shall not reckon itself." (Bamidbar 23:9)*
>
> *(Igrot Kodesh Volume. 27, page 436)*

Raya and her husband separated.

Again, these words are easy to write, difficult to read, and excruciatingly painful to live. Suddenly, at the age of fifty, Raya was alone. No support, no backing, and no family.

But Raya did not let these difficulties break her. Rather, she became stronger. She knew that this is how a Jew must behave, and she refused to compromise.

But there was one thing that really upset her. Now that she was not married, she could not go to the *mikvah*!

Yes, you read right.

Perhaps you have heard (and I am sure that this does not describe you) that there are some women who refuse to keep this special women's *mitzvah*. They can't fathom the greatness of *taharah* and of immersing in the *mikvah*.

But Raya understood.

She understood and felt bad that she had not merited keeping this *mitzvah*. She was not married, and as an unmarried woman she could not go to the *mikvah*.

Raya had almost resigned herself to this lack, just another one of the many things missing in her life, but here Ruchama came into the picture.

"There is still hope," she told her. "You still haven't lived even half of your life (until 120). You can still go to the *mikvah*, if you become a *kallah*!"

Ruchama suggested that Raya write to the Rebbe. A blessing from the Leader of our generation can bring a miracle.

Raya didn't even have the energy to laugh. A *kallah* at age fifty? How ridiculous!

But Hashem saw Raya's devotion to Torah and *mitzvah*s. He decided to put an end to her tribulations. Raya found her soulmate, a partner for life. Mazal Tov!

Against all odds, Raya merited to become a *kallah*! When G-d wants something to happen, statistics don't matter.

She was about to fulfill her dream. Raya was about to get married according to the Law of Moshe and

Israel. And before that, of course, she would immerse in the *mikvah*.

The *mikvah* that Raya went to was located right next to a *shul*. As Raya walked to the *mikvah*, a *Hachnasas Sefer Torah* procession came toward her, as though to greet her! As she walked to the *mikvah*, she was accompanied by a *sefer Torah*, for which she had sacrificed everything, and a *chuppah*, the symbol of the Jewish home she was about to create!

She had truly merited fulfilling the Torah! The circle was complete.

Am Segulah

Rebbetzin Rachel Hendel tells the following story:

One evening, I ran to pick up the phone. It was the Rebbe's *shaliach*, Rabbi Chaim Farro, calling from Manchester, England.

"Will you be home this coming Wednesday?" he asked me.

Although somewhat taken aback, I replied in the affirmative.

"Excellent," he said in Yiddish. "I'll stop in to visit you, together with a couple from our community. It's concerning children."

I was not surprised. Although I am not a "*Baba*" (A Sephardic mystic), nor do I perform miracles, I do tell people about a *segulah* – one that really works. When someone tells me that they are waiting to have children, I suggest this *segulah*, and each time I am amazed anew! My own children were born in its merit, and many couples were saved through it.

What is this *segulah*?

It's simple. The family that is waiting for a salvation should establish a regular *shiur* on Tanya and *Taharas Hamishpacha* in their home. At the conclusion of each *shiur*, the participants should make a *lechaim* on wine or grape juice and bless the couple, using their full Jewish names (including the mother's name). The *segulah* is tried and true. They have the Rebbe's blessing, and, more often than not, they are blessed with offspring. This is true even in cases where the couple has completely despaired of having children.

So as you can see, I wasn't surprised by Rabbi Farro's phone call. But to tell you the truth, I never imagined how it would all end!

This was the first time I'd have the opportunity to welcome guests from England in my house in Tzfas. I even called my daughter to help me get ready! I wanted to serve them a meal fit for royalty. After all, these guests were coming from very far away; perhaps they would give a generous donation to the *tzedakah* fund that I run?

True to English form, Rabbi Farro and the Blums* arrived exactly on time. They must have enjoyed the meal; after all, no one complained. We spoke about all kinds of subjects, and then suddenly, Rabbi Farro raised the subject that they had come from overseas to discuss. "Tell us about children," he requested.

I waited for an explanation, some more details. What exactly did they want to know? How much does a baby weigh? What name to give? Medical advice?

"We want to adopt a child." Mirel Blum dropped the bombshell.

I intuitively felt that there was something more here.

"To adopt? A child? Why?" I spontaneously responded. "Why adopt if you can have your own?"

"A child? Of our own? How??" I could hear the longing and despair in their voices.

"When you do the *segulah*." I said simply. "Organize *shiurim* in *Taharas Hamishpacha* and Tanya in your house. Invite a Chassidishe teacher and serve refreshments." I also mentioned that at the end of the

76

shiur all the participants should make a "*L'chaim*" and bless the couple, mentioning the husband's and wife's names and their mothers' names.

Then I told them about a case where I had personally seen the blessing come to fruition. "Next week," I said, "a very special woman who just gave birth to twins after having done this *segulah* is flying me out to Toronto to see her babies, a boy and a girl! They were born in the merit of this *segulah*."

When I said "twins", an electrical current seemed to pass between the couple. I could sense their yearning. Mirel was no longer able to hold herself back. "I don't want an abstract child!" she cried from the depth of her heart. "These are just words and promises. I want a real child. Bring me a child, RIGHT NOW!"

They had heard rumors that when I convince women not to have abortions, I arrange for them to give their children up for adoption. I quickly set them straight. I had never dealt with such things, and I certainly didn't intend to start now. But I also felt that it's Divine Providence that had given them such an idea so that they would come to me to hear about the *segulah*.

But they were not convinced. They wanted to leave with a child in their arms, or at least with a document promising them one in the near future. But, as you already know, that was not possible. It hurt me to see their disappointment, but there was really nothing I could do for them except to refer them to a friend who could instruct them about applying for adoption in Israel.

As they were standing at the door, about to leave, I said, "Mirel, please follow my advice. It's worth your while. What can happen? Try. At the maximum, it will work."

The following week, I flew to Toronto, and from there, to the Rebbe in Crown Heights. I asked the Rebbe for brachos for many people, including the Blum family. Over the next few months, I prayed for

Mirel while lighting the Shabbos candles.

Six months later, I was looking through some papers and found Mirel's number. I phoned to see how she was. There was no answer, so I left a message.

The following day, Mirel called me back.

"How are you?" I asked warmly.

"Do you remember what you said to me? 'Why do you want to adopt a child?'" She was very emotional. "You were right. I'm expecting! We're waiting for our own child!"

"You did the *segulah*?" I asked.

"Of course," she replied. "As soon as I got back to Manchester, I organized *shiurim* on the laws of *Taharas Hamishpacha* and Tanya, and they are still going on. I'm now in my fifth month, Baruch Hashem."

I was thrilled and I waited to hear the good news.

Once again, I misplaced Mirel's number. She never called.

Over *Shavuos*, I merited to be in New York with the Rebbe. While I was there, I gave classes in English. At the end of one of the lectures, a girl came up to me and said: "A friend of my Mom in Manchester knows you."

I only knew one woman in Manchester. Mirel Blum!

The girl continued: "My mother delivers *shiurim* at her house."

"And how is Mirel?" I asked.

"Didn't you hear? She gave birth to a girl! Everyone in Manchester is talking about your *segulah* and the miracle that occurred. Now other couples who don't have children also want *shiurim* to be given in their house. Since then there has been a huge demand for my Mom's lectures, and the miracles continue!"

&

"There is no need to worry about financial burdens

since G-d provides sustenance and livelihood to everyone.

He takes upon Himself the responsibility for

supporting the father and the mother

and all of their offspring.

When an additional child is born,

its sustenance is "born" together with him."

(adapted from Rebbe's speech from 1980)

"It's no longer relevant"

Yehudit, an experienced *Taharas Hamishpacha* counselor, tells her story:

Standing outside my front door one morning was a woman that I had never seen before. I sensed that there was something different about her. She wasn't like the young, shining brides who usually come to my *shiurim*.

The Israeli Rabbinate requires all brides marrying according to Jewish law to take a compulsory course on the laws of *Taharas Hamishpacha*. The brides often listen, and then leave. Their minds are elsewhere, planning the details of their upcoming wedding. But this women was different. She seemed worried and distressed. Not at all like the glowing, happy *kallah*s that I was used to.

We spoke together for a few minutes. I was trying to be nice, but, for some strange reason, she wasn't. I felt her pain as she told me that she was happily married, but that they did not yet have children.

So why was she coming to me?

It just so happened that a friend of her husband told him that he had read that keeping the *mitzvah* of *Taharas Hamishpacha* is a *segulah* for having children. And she wanted to try.

But if I had expected her to be one of my most eager students, thirsting for knowledge, I would have been mistaken. She sat across from me, frozen-faced, without showing that she understood a word that I said. It seemed that she was constantly asking herself: "What am I doing here?" and waiting for the opportunity to rush out the door.

At the end of the second lesson, she impatiently asked me, "How many more meetings are there?"

Yes, it was rather insulting, but I was able to separate my personal feelings from the task at hand and answered with a smile.

During our third lesson, I sensed that a narrow crack had formed in the ice. She seemed to be somewhat interested as she realized that keeping these laws was actually doable. By the time we finished all the *shiurim*, she promised me wholeheartedly that she intended to keep the *halachos*. This time, we were both smiling as we parted.

Several months later…

I regularly invite the women who learned with me to a refresher course in *Taharas Hamishpacha*. So I phoned this woman, and after some polite chitchat I asked her if she was still keeping the laws.

"No," she replied. "Not anymore."

I felt the bile rise in my throat; after so much effort.

"But didn't you promise to try?"

"Yes," she continued, "but right now it's not necessary. We're expecting a child."[1]

---

1 During pregnancy, a woman does not menstruate and usually does not have to go to the *mikvah* until after the birth.

A Cupboard like The Ark of the Holy Covenant

Rebbetzin Rivka Gorelik told the following story:

In the 1960s, we lived in Tashkent, the capital of the former Soviet state of Uzbekistan when it was a challenge to use mikvah, and it was illegal to have one.

Our house was on a quiet side street. We had added a porch near the wall that we shared with the neighbors, and between the house and this porch we installed a huge cupboard that ran all along the wall.

The cupboard contained shelves that we used for storage, except for one double door that led to another door. That door led to the *mikvah*.

How did we build a *mikvah* inside our home? Well, we hired workers. Obviously they weren't Jewish. They had no idea what they were building and it was better that way.

The *otzar* was built by one team of workers, while a second team built the *mikvah* itself. They thought they were building a swimming pool.

According to Jewish Law, the *mikvah*'s walls and floor must be completely watertight; try explaining that to the workers. When we tried, they responded that there was really no need. For a swimming pool, simple waterproofing is sufficient. "What's the big deal if a few drops of water disappear?" they argued. "Most of the water will stay inside.

Our grandfather lived with us. He was elderly and not in the best of health. We explained to the workers that his physician had prescribed special mineral baths for him. The concentration of minerals had to be

exact, and if even a small amount of water drained away, it would change the concentration and that, G-d forbid, could harm our grandfather.
How could anyone argue with such logic?!

We heated the *mikvah* with natural gas. The water was changed very late at night, so that the neighbors would not notice. Despite the danger, the women came, quietly, taking care that no one saw them. They stealthily entered the cupboard, and when they came out, they were pure.

That simple cupboard bears witness to the fact that Am *Yisrael* will never allow the forces of evil to break its covenant with Hashem.

ଈ

"A marriage is not only the beginning of a partnership,

but the beginning of a union, where both partners become one

and are united for life in order to set up an 'everlasting edifice',

as mentioned in the text of the wedding blessings.

Therefore it is clear that everything should be done in order

to assure the maximum degree of compliance with the Will of G-d,

the Creator and the Master of the Universe and of man.

G-d's providence extends to everyone individually."

(Letters From The Rebbe, Vol 1. page 173)

The Connecting Thread

Chana* tells her story:

Our story begins in Russia. In 1980 I gave birth to a baby girl. She lived for just three days. Three years later I delivered a baby boy. We had the pleasure of raising him for just eighteen days. Yes, we lost this child as well. We were shattered and heartbroken, unable to recover.

In 1988, I was hospitalized because of a danger to my unborn child. There was no choice but to induce labor. His lungs were not sufficiently developed, and we lost him, too.

We underwent innumerable medical tests. Some were painful, and some were even more painful. The result were: we had a 25% risk of my giving birth to a child that wouldn't live.

My husband and I emigrated from the USSR and moved to the land of endless opportunity, the United States of America. We assumed that the doctors there would be more optimistic, or may be come up with some treatment solutions, but this was not the case. They, too, told us that according to the statistics, one out of four children born to us wouldn't survive.

As for reality, we had already lost three out of three children. Should we continue trying? The private doctor we asked thought that we should not. "Adopt a child," he advised. "Why go through such emotional suffering?"

"But there's a 75% chance that everything will be okay!" I cried. I longed for a child. How could I just give up on my dream like that?

"Yes, in theory there's a 75% chance," the doctor replied. "But what happens in reality, you know better, or rather, worse than I do."

We left him, broken and confused.

Like many of the immigrants from the USSR, we didn't know much about Yiddishkeit. We were ignorant of the basics. When friends brought us a mezuzah as a gift, we had no idea what that strange elongated object was for.

"This will guard your home," our friends explained. We had no idea where to put it, or what to use it for.

I phoned a friend, who told me that before placing the mezuzah on our front door, I should bring it to an expert Sofer Sta"m (one who is qualified to write Torah scrolls, *mezuzos* and *tefillin*), to make sure that it was kosher.

We looked for a Sofer Sta"m and found new friends.

Life is full of surprises!

The *sofer* invited us for a Shabbos meal, and we gratefully accepted. When we learned that they did not drive on Shabbos, we parked our car a few streets away from their house and walked the rest of the way.

That was the first of many visits. We became almost like family.

They heard about our efforts to bring a healthy child into the world and really felt our pain. They wanted to help us. With tears in our eyes, we told them about our difficult journey and the heartbreaking decision we had to make.

"Have you tried asking Hashem?" We were surprised at the *sofer's* strange question. "Six hundred and thirteen hidden strands tie us to the Creator of the world," he explained.

We listened.

"When we do a *mitzvah* here, in the physical world," he continued, "we attach ourselves to one of these strands. There are five threads that are the main conduits: Shabbos, Purity, a *Chuppah*, Bris and Kashrus. I suggest you start with these *mitzvah*s."

We started to keep Shabbos and *Taharas Hamishpacha*. My husband, who was close to forty years of age, underwent a Bris.

Now that we were holding three strong strands, I became pregnant. I had to stay in bed the entire time so I would not miscarry.

The baby was born at full term, but after five months, he passed away.

My husband broke down completely. "Enough!" he almost yelled. "No more experiments!"

But I was not ready to give up. I would never forgive myself if I had not done everything possible to have a healthy child.

We were holding three strands: Shabbos, *Mikvah* and *Bris,* we added one more, a kosher *chuppah*.

Two weeks before Pesach I had a crazy idea. At least my husband thought it was crazy. "Let's kasher the kitchen." I said. "Now is the perfect time!"

My husband couldn't understand what had come over me; It was a spontaneous decision, yet a firm one.

That year, we had a kosher Pesach.

A month later, I discovered that I was pregnant. Eight months later I gave birth to a beautiful, healthy girl!

What school would we send her to?

What education would she receive?

These were no longer questions for us. We were trying to hold as many strands as possible. We are doing our job in this world, and the Creator will do His part and send us His blessings.

The proof is in this story.

80

"And I shall sprinkle upon you pure water and you shall be purified,
and I shall put My Spirit among you…
and you shall be a people unto Me
and I shall be your G-d"
(Yechezkel 36:25)

What is there to be Ashamed of?

A married couple having a *chuppah* can result in some amazing situations.

Here's one:

A middle-aged woman came to Yehudit, a seasoned *kallah* teacher, to request that she teach her the *halachos* of *Taharas Hamishpacha*. She was in a happy second marriage and successfully raising a beautiful blended family. She and her husband decided that it was time to bring the Creator of the World into their shared lives and have a proper, kosher *chuppah*.

They wanted a simple affair. No glitter, nothing fancy. Just a festive meal shared with close family members, the Rabbi and the *kallah* teacher, Yehudit. On the night of the event, everything was ready: the *kesubah* was signed, the wine, cup, and veil were waiting, yet the Rabbi was stalling.

What was he waiting for?

A minyan and two men not related to the bride or groom to act as witnesses for the ceremony.

How could they invite strangers to this small, intimate family affair? Should they just pull strangers off the street?

"Perhaps we can have the *chuppah* without a minyan? What would be so terrible? We have seven men already, just three men missing," someone asked.

The *kallah*'s sixteen-year-old son solved the problem. "I'll call three of my friends and invite them to the wedding."

"You won't be embarrassed?" the groom asked. After all, how many sixteen-year-olds have parents who are getting married?

"Embarrassed?" the boy asked. "Why should I be embarrassed? My friends' parents are all getting divorced. But mine, they're getting married! Why should I be embarrassed about that?"

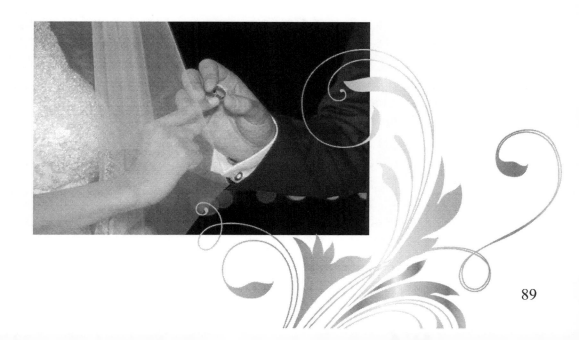

I am an Intellectual

Rita tells her story:

I was born in Ukraine. My family moved to New York when I was seventeen. Over the years, I slowly started to keep Torah and *mitzvah*s. But I never became what you'd call ultra-orthodox. I still wore jeans and t-shirts, and hung out with the same crowd. I combined a life of Torah with American culture.

I received my education in one of America's topnotch universities and graduated as a physicist. Today I am married, and we are raising our children to follow the American dream – to get a good education and then earn a nice living as a professional – combined with a life of Torah observance.

As are most scientists, I am much more intellectual than emotional. And as an intellectual, I found it very difficult to understand all the seemingly petty details involved in keeping the *mitzvah* of *Taharas Hamishpacha*. My brain rules my heart.

Yes, I've heard the nice explanations, and the even nicer stories; how keeping this *mitzvah* improves one's married life, and how much it is a *segulah* for miracles.

But I was never impressed by miracle stories. And emotions, well, I'm certainly not swayed by feelings. But eventually, I realized that not everything can be understood intellectually. Some things need to be experienced before they can be understood.

Can anyone explain how an orange tastes to someone who has never eaten citrus? Can anyone explain the enormity of a mother's love for her newborn child? There are no words that can express what excitement, jealousy, admiration feels like to one who has never experienced it.

The *mitzvah* of *Taharah* is one of those hidden, inner phenomena that no words can adequately explain. To understand it, it must first be experienced.

I experienced it.

I, who was so proud of my rational thinking, who viewed everything through pure intellect, experienced the incredible joy that is an integral part of this special *mitzvah*.

To those women reading this book that are also unimpressed by emotional stories, let me say this to you: Try it. See for yourself. You have to actually do the *mitzvah* to experience the results.

Believe me, you won't be sorry.

I promise you!

ॐ

"...Taharat Hamishpaha - by keeping the laws of niddah, purification and immersion, which was given to Jewish women, she is bringing purity and holiness into her family life. By observing this mitzvah she'll merit to have good and healthy children, their bodies and their souls will be whole and complete; children, who are going in the ways of Torah and mitzvos and bringing nachas and happiness to their parents."

(Rebbe's Sichos in Hebrew, Vol.2, page 261)

A Marriage Saved

This story occurred many years ago. There was a young couple who had a very unhappy marriage, and they decided to divorce. The wife's mother, who lived in Israel, was devastated by this decision, and she flew in to New York to speak personally to her children. "They were determined to split up, as they had neither love nor respect for one another", Mrs. Sara Karmely of Kew Gardens, New York, relates.

"I drove the mother to 770 for prayers with the Lubavitcher Rebbe. This was before the years that the Rebbe would distribute "dollars." I wrote a note for the young couple, saying that they were seeking a divorce, and submitted it to the Rebbe's office prior to the afternoon prayers. We stood in the lobby of 770 and merited to see the Rebbe as he went in and out of his office to pray.

After the prayers were over, I told the mother that we would be going home, when all of a sudden the door leading to the Rebbe's room opened, and Rabbi Groner (the Rebbe's secretary) emerged, and told me: "You have an answer to your note."

He showed me the Rebbe's holy handwriting on the note that I had written. He had written for the couple to "keep family purity meticulously". I was so excited!

I immediately drove to the home of Chana, (the wife) and told her what the Rebbe had advised.

"Oh no, it's too late" she answered, hopelessly, "we have already decided that it's better to separate."

I was able to convince them to at least try to listen to the Rebbe's instruction, saying that it was worth it, and that there was no harm in trying. She came to learn with me, and I taught her all the laws, and she promised to go to the *mikvah* and keep what she was supposed to.

Two days before her *mikvah* night, she called me and asked me a question.

"Can I go to the *mikvah* with fake nails?" she asked. "I went and had fake nails applied, and I really don't want to have to remove them. Can I go with them still on me?"

Of course, I could have answered her that she definitely had to have them removed, as they formed an interposition between her and the *mikvah* waters, and would therefore not be permitted. However, I told her that she should ask a competent rabbi, who would be able to advise her what to do.

"Please, would you ask for me?" she said. So I did. I made sure to tell the rabbi about her particular situation, that she had never ever observed the commandment of family purity, and this would be her first time keeping it.

After taking everything into consideration, the rabbi said that she would be allowed this time only to go to the *mikvah* with the fake nails, but that she should make sure to clean them well, and remove any nail polish on them.

"This special dispensation is because she would not go otherwise, and also once she starts to keep this commandment, she would continue to do so," the rabbi said. Of course, it is imperative to emphasize that this allowance, is ONLY FOR THIS WOMAN AND NOT FOR ANYONE ELSE. Only a competent rabbi can give permission for such a thing. I duly told Chana the rabbi's decision and also informed the *mikvah* lady, so she should not question the matter.

Time went by, and the *mikvah* lady asked me one day: "Mrs. Karmely, how come you told me about that lady who had permission to go to the *mikvah* with fake nails? Did you know that she actually had

had them removed before she came to the *mikvah*?"

I was surprised, to say the least, and I asked Chana what had happened that she had them taken off.

"You had asked me if you could keep them on, and I got permission for you to do so, and then you had them removed. What made you do that?" I asked, curiously.

Her answer made me very happy!

"You told me that the Rebbe said that I should keep family purity meticulously," she said earnestly. "So I decided that if I am to keep this commandment, I should really keep it properly, otherwise I would not feel right. The Rebbe knows more than I do."

This is a true story. Chana is my cousin, and I know for a fact that her marriage was a disaster. However, the total change in her marriage after she started to keep the commandment of family purity was dramatic and amazing! She not only did NOT get divorced, but she and her husband have become totally observant, keeping Shabbat, kosher, and family purity. She wears a wig and dresses modestly. He has grown a beard and learns Torah with great happiness and joy. They made *aliyah* to Israel shortly after, and have a marriage that is exemplary, full of respect and love.

Most importantly, Chana finally was able to conceive and has four beautiful children. One of the problems that she had was the fact that they were unable to have children before she started to keep family purity.

Although this commandment is a super-rational commandment, something that we cannot understand with our finite knowledge, the rewards are obvious - improved family harmony, and the blessings of healthy children. Surely this commandment is truly a gift from G-d to His children, given to us in His great kindness and wisdom. It is a blueprint for a G-dly marriage, a marriage that is true and everlasting".

Immersion with Self-Sacrifice

Many Lubavitcher Chassidim in Russia fled in the direction of Asia during World War II. They settled, partly, in Tashkent, Uzbekistan. Rebbetzin Frida Sossonkin related:

In the summer of 1962, the Communist government suddenly closed and sealed the *mikvah* in Tashkent that was located in the backyard of the synagogue. Several weeks later I heard that there was a *mikvah* available. I asked my friend about the rumor and she told me that when I would need it, she would go with me.

The night that I had to go to the *mikvah,* I prepared myself and off we went. Soon we came to the backyard of the synagogue. My friend called the woman who used to work in the *mikvah* and lived in the same courtyard.

She went to the side of the old *mikvah*, lifted a cover on the ground, and uncovered a well (a *mikvah* is kosher only when the water is connected with a "living" source of water). Since Tashkent is in the mountains where it seldom rains, they had to dig very deep to make the well.

It was summertime and the rabbis said we could use this well as a temporary *mikvah* until they could find a secret place to build a permanent one. They put a table on the bottom of the well, and connected two long ladders and put them on the table in the well. The temporary *mikvah* was ready.

When I stepped down, the cold air of the well hit me. As my toes touched the water I automatically pulled out my foot because the water was ice cold. I cupped some water in my hands and wet my feet with the cold water. I tried again to put my foot in the water, but it was impossible. I decided to give up, to leave the well without immersing myself. I knew that it was not proper, but I would wait until a proper *mikvah* was built.

At that moment I heard two other women entering the yard to use the *mikvah*. From their talking I recognized the voice of my friend Zlata.

I realized that if they saw me coming out of the *mikvah* without having immersed they would go straight home. I now felt three times the responsibility I had felt before these women came. I decided to immerse in this *mikvah* no matter what.

I had once heard that when one of the great Sages studied Torah, he would bite his fingers in deep concentration until blood would come, and because he was so involved in his studies, he didn't feel the pain and he didn't see the blood. I knew that if I could completely distract my attention and concentrate on something else, I would not feel the cold and I would be able to immerse my entire body in the ice cold water.

And so, I began to think about one day in my life - 21 Shevat, 5711 (1951). My husband, Reb Asher (of blessed memory) had been arrested by the KGB nine months before. The KGB ran a powerful and cruel regime and this was its most bitter year. They arrested thousands of innocent people, especially Lubavitcher Chassidim.

During the first month, I was able to bring kosher food for him three times (once every ten days). When I came the fourth time with the food, I was told that he had been sent away to another city for interrogation. Where? They "didn't know"...

The next day I received a note to come to the interrogator on Friday. I went. Finally in the afternoon they brought me to the interrogator who interrogated me for four hours. And then, he allowed me to leave! I was able to come home and light my Shabbat candles on time. The next Friday they interrogated me again. During that year they arrested many Chassidim and I was very worried about what would happen to my children. Every time I went out of my house I knew that a KGB agent was following me. I could not meet, or talk to my friends. I could only talk to G-d.

Eight months passed and I still didn't know the whereabouts of my husband. I didn't know if he was still alive. Nine months after my husband was arrested, on Shevat 21, 5711, I lost my two children in a fire.

Standing on the steps of the ladder, down in the well, deeply engrossed in the events and emotions of that day, I no longer "felt my body" and I jumped into the water. I didn't feel the cold. I knew how to swim, and I wanted to swim out of the water to the surface of the well, but I couldn't because there wasn't any air in my lungs, and I couldn't breathe. I begged G-d to help me and to save my life for the sake of my husband and our third (now only) child (my husband came home in 1956 and in 1957 our son, until 120, was born). I suddenly found myself on the surface of the water.

I finished immersing and came out of the well. I touched my body and it was ice cold. Only slowly did my blood begin to circulate. When I came out, Zlata went down into the well. I stopped to listen. Suddenly, a cry came out from the well: "It's too cold. I can't take it. I'm going out." Then she began to weep, and so did I, and still weeping, she immersed herself. She came out and said that she would never come to this *mikvah* again. The other young woman went quietly into the *mikvah*, immersed herself quietly and came out.

I was proud and relieved. After that night, Zlata permitted the rabbis to build a *mikvah* in her yard, and with G-d's help, we also built a *mikvah* in our kitchen. The building of our *mikvah* took place with much self-sacrifice and many miracles.

Even though the Communists (may their names and memories be erased) closed the only *mikvah* in Tashkent, with G-d's help and with the self-sacrifice of many Jews, we kept the commandment of family purity and we were able to build two secret *mikva'ot*.

In 1964, thank G-d, we miraculously got out of Russia. We left our home to a Lubavitcher family. They promised us they would take care of the *mikvah,* and the *mikvah* remained open for women.

In 1967 there were two earthquakes in Tashkent. All the buildings around our home collapsed. But our house with the *mikvah* remained standing.

છ

"Great is the merit of this mitzvah of building a kosher mikveh…

G-d will bless all those involved in this with living offspring

and will also bring general redemption

to all Israel (to all the Jewish people)."

(from Rebbe's letter)

Clear Eyes

An elderly woman was sitting on a bench on Eastern Parkway in New York, enjoying the warm rays of the sun on a chilly winter day. A young mother with a baby carriage sat down next to her, pushing the carriage back and forth to the enjoyment of her baby.

The two women started a conversation, chatting about various matters. After some time, the elderly woman opened up her purse, and took out a picture that she handed to the young woman. It was a picture of her family - herself, her husband and her children.

"I don't know why I'm telling you this," the woman said, "but I'd like to tell you something. We have been living in this neighborhood for years, but we are not part of the Lubavitcher community.

"A couple of years ago my husband and I asked for permission to meet the Rebbe in a private audience, since we have a great deal of respect for him and we considered that it would be a great honor to meet him in person. Among other matters that were discussed at our meeting was this picture of our family that I showed to the Rebbe. He looked at the picture, pointed to one of the girls (our first-born daughter) and said: 'This daughter was born out of self-sacrifice for family purity.'

"And this was true. I'll tell you what had happened. We were married in Poland a short time before the outbreak of World War II and we managed to escape the Germans by fleeing to Russia and then we went as far as the Arctic Ocean. When the time arrived for me to have a ritual bath, I went to the sea, since there was no *mikvah* in the entire area. The ocean was stormy and huge waves crashed onto the shore.

"I threw myself into the water without really knowing whether I would ever return from the stormy sea. Afterwards our first daughter was born.

"The Rebbe saw at first glance that she was born out of self-sacrifice for family purity."

The young woman remained seated for a long time afterwards on the bench, contemplating the old woman's story. She realized the greatness of self-sacrifice for the keeping of Torah and its commandments, the enormous importance of keeping the laws of family purity and how the adherence to these laws has such a great impact that someone with sharp and clear eyes can see on the face of that person, in what manner he or she was born.

Dryan mikvah, Palo Alto, CA

Jewish Legacy

by Laura Barnes

I met Bronya Shaffer many years ago when my husband and I were about to celebrate our 50th anniversary. She was a guest speaker at a women's Torah study group and she taught us about *mikvah*. Following her talk, I asked her to tell me more and at her suggestion I decided to do this ceremony prior to our anniversary celebration. Bronya took me to a *mikvah* in a small town in Upstate New York. After I immersed myself in the *mikvah*, she presented me with flowers, a bottle of wine and a pair of candles. I can't say why, but tears began to flow and I felt like something happened to me that never happened before. I felt connected to all the generations of Jewish women, past and future. I asked Bronya how I could ever repay her. She said: "Take this gift and when the time comes you will pass it on to someone else. Maybe even your granddaughter some day."

Last year, my granddaughter introduced me to her Jewish fiancé. I was so overwhelmed with happiness. I said I would like to give her a special gift. I took her to the *mikvah*, which I had prearranged, and I showered her with flowers and led her to the *mikvah* waters. She cried and cried.

I told her, "One day you will have a daughter and she will grow up and get married to a Jewish man. I want you to pass on this gift to her, the gift of *mikvah*. It's for her to pass on to her daughter and so we will forever pass on this gift to the Jewish women in our family."

This is my experience of the *mikvah*. Thank you for allowing me to share it.

The Book and a Miracle

Luba Perlov tells the following story:

This story began in 2012 with the wonderful news that we were going to welcome a new addition to our family. But then we found out that something was wrong with my pregnancy. In despair, we wrote a letter to the Rebbe, asking for his blessing and for his advice as to what we could do to assure that this pregnancy would continue and that I would give birth to a healthy child. We inserted our letter at random into one of the books of the Igrot Kodesh, the collection of the Rebbe's letters.

The answer came out in volume 23, page 331. We were happy to read the Rebbe's blessing at the end of one of the letters: "...Let it will be G-d's will that the pregnancy will be successful and that a healthy baby will be born in a good and happy moment." The beginning of the letter contained a list of the Rebbe's instructions. In one of them, the Rebbe stated that he wanted ME (I took this letter personally, although it was written to another person over fifty-two years ago) to encourage at least three married Jewish couples to keep the *mitzvah* of Family Purity.

Family Purity certainly wasn't the type of topic I could discuss with friends, let alone with strangers! Although I in the past I taught some women the laws of *Taharas Hamishpacha*, it was always at their initiative, not mine.

Then I recalled that Family Purity was the very first *mitzvah* that I consciously started keeping! Maybe that was a sign from Heaven that this *mitzvah* was my special mission in this world?! And who would know this better than the Rebbe?! Now, in my desperate situation, when my life and my unborn baby's life were in jeopardy I couldn't procrastinate! I had to start immediately!

It suddenly dawned on me that although I would have difficulty speaking directly to women to convince them to keep the laws of *Taharas Hamishpacha*, I could accomplish the same thing, and even more, through publishing a book. I decided to publish a collection of personal stories about the *mikvah* in my native language, Russian. Like myself, my Russian Jewish sisters grew up in anti-religious and anti-Semitic country. Most of them were never given the opportunity to learn about their heritage. With Hashem's help, I hoped that a book like this would inspire and encourage these women to start keeping the amazing and powerful *mitzvah* of *Taharas Hamishpacha*.

But me? Write a book? I'm an artist and an illustrator, not a professional writer. Where would I find all the necessary material? How would I pay for the publishing? Who would do the typesetting and layout? And besides, I had young children at home and was trying to cope with a high-risk pregnancy; was this really the right time to start such a project?

I had no solutions, yet miraculously, I found myself in the midst of producing this book. Not everything was new material. I had written some articles on this topic. So I began interviewing women and translating material from Hebrew and English into Russian. And slowly, click by click, I did something completely new for me; I learned a computer program for preparing a book for publication.

Meanwhile, tests confirmed that my doctor's worries were correct. I had a rare pregnancy complication that endangered both my life and the life of my unborn child.

The doctor, who had scheduled a planned C-section, panicked. I realized that I must find a different doctor quickly. I didn't have much time. Again, I wrote to the Rebbe and felt the power of his blessing.

103

Friends and friends of friends helped me to contact the head of the maternity department in the hospital where my surgery had been scheduled to take place. He wasn't accepting new patients, but he made an exception for me. He explained that my condition was so rare that a doctor could complete his entire career without encountering such a patient. So he was thrilled at the opportunity to treat me!

Throughout my pregnancy, every time there was a change in my condition I wrote to the Rebbe, and each time I received an answer and blessing that fitted my question exactly. One time, the Rebbe's response was in volume 11, page 162. Together with blessings for a successful birth was advice to check *mezuzos* and *tefillin*. So of course we made sure to immediately have ours checked by a professional *sofer*. The *mezuzos* were fine, but both of my husband's *tefillin* were unusable and not able to be repaired. Of course, we purchased a new pair.

Meanwhile, obviously thanks to the Rebbe's constant support, the book miraculously progressed rapidly. It was Divine Providence that, while collecting material, I became acquainted with Ruchama Rosenshtein. Through the Rebbe's assignment she established the volunteer organization *Apirion* to promote *Taharas Hamishpacha* and Jewish marriage. Thanks to the many women who responded to her request for help, *Apirion* covered the cost of publication.

Although I was basically on bed rest, I was busy interviewing women, writing articles, translating from Hebrew and English, typing, designing the book cover, consulting often with rabbis and preparing the book files to print. I certainly learned a lot!

Actually, it was a real team effort. Although we live on different sides of the globe – I'm in California, and Ruchama Rosenshtein and her friends are in Israel – we were working together almost 24 hours a day to get this book done. Despite all our efforts, we all felt that the book had a power of its own, that we were not the ones writing it.

And yes, it was a miracle! It took just six weeks from the moment I came up with the idea of writing a book, until the Russian language edition of Let it Stay Between Us was published! I was still pregnant when the book was published.

When I went to the hospital, I took some of the books with me, so that if I'd meet a Russian-speaking Jewish doctor or nurse I'd be able to give it to him or her. And believe it or not, I actually had the opportunity! One nurse got the book for her mother. She wanted her mother to go to the *mikvah*!

I was hospitalized for about five weeks. During that difficult time, I often wrote to the Rebbe, and each time I read the response I was overwhelmed with emotion. I often found myself crying from gratitude and a sense of closeness. I believe that anyone who has received such accurate and direct answers from the Rebbe, feels likewise. It was obvious to me that the Rebbe was supporting me, and that he was at my side. His answers and blessings became an integral part of my life story.

My medical condition was far from stable. My life and my unborn baby's life were in danger. Every day the blood bank defrosted close to a dozen pints of blood in case the situation worsened and I would suddenly need it, G-d forbid.

As the pregnancy progressed and my due date grew closer, there was a disagreement between my doctor and the doctors in the NICU, who would be responsible for the care of my baby. On one hand, an early delivery would endanger the baby, but on the other hand, my situation was life threatening, and the earlier I gave birth, the less chance I had of developing serious complications. Several times, the doctors gave me a delivery date, but then they would change it to a different and earlier, date. It was very confusing, yet each time I wrote to the Rebbe, I did not receive an appropriate response until the Rebbe recommended that I bring both doctors together and demand a mutual decision. Yes, that is literally how it appeared in the Rebbe's letter.

I followed the Rebbe's advice and invited both doctors to my room. Together, they came up with a mutually agreed upon date. I immediately informed the Rebbe and asked for a blessing. I was amazed at his response. Although the original letter was written years ago to a woman I don't know, I felt as if the Rebbe wrote it directly to me, now! The letter discussed in detail the same type of operation that I was about to have and included blessings for a full recovery.

Meanwhile, I had unwillingly become a hospital celebrity. Doctors from different departments heard about my case and came to see me out of curiosity. I asked one of these visiting physicians if he was planning to be present in the operating room. With a smile, he responded, "unfortunately not. The tickets were all sold out."

My doctor, who was head of the department, planned my surgery like a military operation, down to the very last detail. Everyone present knew exactly what was expected of him at any given moment. Later on, my doctor told me that during the surgery twenty-three physicians and one intern were taking care of me.

I felt, that in addition to all the technical preparation, it was necessary for the doctor to prepare himself spiritually for the surgery. After all, he had to be a part of the miracle. So although my doctor is not Jewish, I hoped to find the proper words to convey the importance of the Rebbe's blessing.

I wrote the Rebbe to ask how to convey this to the doctor. His response was in volume 8, page 145:

'… I received your letter from 19 Shevat. You wrote that you are hospitalized and under medical supervision, and described your worrisome condition. But as it is known, each person must trust in G-d who is the Healer of all flesh who performs miracles. As your trust in G-d increases, your

medical condition will improve. Together with this, the holy Torah teaches us that a doctor has G-d's permission to heal, that he is an emissary of the Healer of all flesh, and in order to strengthen trust in Hashem and to add Hashem's blessing, one must also increase his observance of Torah and mitzvahs, each person according to his position and situation. In addition it is not enough that he be involved solely with himself, rather, he should encourage those around him, for surely he can influence them to some degree, and encourage them in both trust in Hashem and increasing Torah and mitzvah observance. And G-d's measures will be accordingly: whoever put his efforts into improving the spiritual and physical health of his fellow Jews, G-d's reward will be many times greater. Let it be His will that you'll report good news about all that is mentioned above, with blessing."

The next time, when my doctor came to my room, I told him about the Rebbe and that the Rebbe sent him a message. I explained to him that he is Hashem's emissary and that if he puts his trust fully in Hashem, Hashem will help him to make the surgery a success.

The doctor listened closely to what I was telling him. He had always seemed so confident in himself, yet now I could sense his worry and concern. I understood what I was facing. I have no doubt that without the Rebbe's support, I would have started panicking. But the Rebbe had strengthened my faith and given me so much support that I was positive that everything would work out fine.

Being that it is a widespread custom to have cards with Psalm 121 in the delivery room, several of the doctors and nurses already knew about it! It is a *segulah* for the mother to have an easier delivery, and is placed in the newborn's crib as a protection for the baby. It's also our first step of giving our child a

Jewish education. The first thing the newborn sees are the pure letters of *Tehillim*, and that will leave a deep impression on his or her soul.

I had brought cards with me and had no difficulty convincing the medical staff to allow me to place them in the baby's incubator. After all, they wanted me to stay calm and happy.

Of course I wrote to the Rebbe before the surgery. In addition to a blessing and review of the details of my operation (!), the Rebbe instructed me to imagine the image of "my righteous grandfather" during any unpleasant procedure.

To be honest I don't really remember either of my grandfathers: one was killed in World War II, and the other passed away when I was very young. So I decided that the Rebbe would be my grandfather.

There was a problem with the anesthesia during the surgery, and the Rebbe's advice was very useful. I closed my eyes and tried to focus on memories of pictures and videos of the Rebbe. I immediately felt better.

My story has a happy ending. In a good and happy hour, I gave birth to a beautiful baby girl. The surgery lasted for four hours. The outcome was much better than what the doctors had expected. In the course of the surgery, the doctors were afraid for my life and for my unborn baby's life. They assumed that I would need to be put into an induced coma and receive numerous blood transfusions. Instead, within a few hours I was up and walking! The doctor himself - and not me! – described it as a miracle. The Rebbe saved my life, and my baby's life.

This book that you are now holding in your hands is a part of that miracle. Thanks to this book, baruch Hashem, my friends and I have been able to influence women to keep the *mitzvah* of Family Purity, bringing happiness and blessing to numerous families.

But now that I've accomplished the Rebbe's wish, I cannot just sit back and rest. The Rebbe is constantly letting me know that my job has just begun!

That's why, my dear reader, when you learn about the *mitzvah* of *Taharas Hamishpacha* and go to the *mikvah* (as I'm sure you will), please pass it on. Tell your relatives and friends. And if you are currently not able to keep this *mitzvah*, help others to keep it. Hashem is infinite and He has infinite blessings for everyone.

Mikvah Simcha Yisroel, California

Full Circle

Luba Perlov tells the following story.

Baruch and I grew up in Odessa, Ukraine. When we decided to get married, we encountered a serious obstacle. Because Baruch's USSR citizenship had been taken away (which was a standard procedure for anyone who expressed a desire to emigrate in the 1990s), we were unable to have a civil marriage. Yet, for me to be able to leave the USSR together with Baruch, I had to be his legal wife. Baruch had already booked a flight to Israel. The Iron Curtain could close again at any moment, so we had to take advantage of this window of opportunity. Who knew if we'd ever have another chance?

A family friend advised us to travel to Moscow, to the Israeli representatives stationed at the Netherlands embassy, since at that time there were no diplomatic relations between Israel and the Soviet Union.

It was the middle of the winter. Moscow was covered with a deep snow. At six o'clock in the morning, we found ourselves standing outside in the bitter cold, waiting in a long line that extended for a couple of blocks, leading to the Netherlands embassy. We kept stamping our feet to warm ourselves, yet it would be another two hours before the embassy would even open! A CNN truck with a crane was standing in front of a gate as journalists were getting ready for a big shoot.

At 8 o'clock sharp, the gate opened wide and hundreds of people who just seconds before were standing orderly in line, now started pushing and shoving to get inside. Baruch and I joined the crowd. Within seconds the embassy's inner courtyard was packed.

We somehow managed to push our way into the building. We found ourselves packed like sardines into a narrow corridor as we waited our turn outside a little white door. Hours passed, people went in and out, but the hot and stuffy room remained just as crowded.

Finally, when we were next in line, we heard an announcement: "Reception is over for today!"

People slowly started to leave. Soon the corridor was deserted, but we remained standing in shock and disbelief in front of the little white door.

The door opened slightly and a man with a large nose poked his head out. "Are you here for a personal matter?" he asked

"Yes, we responded in the unison.

"For a VERY personal matter?" he asked again.

"Yes! VERY personal!" Baruch and I echoed, our voices shaking.

Then the man disappeared from view and an index finger poked out to signal us to enter.

We entered the small room. The man heard our story and gave one, and only one, word of advice. "Make a *chuppah*. When you come to the consulate next time, bring the *kesubah*. In Israel, we view it as an official document and will register you as a married couple. Just shake the *kesubah* over the heads of everyone in the crowd so that we'll see it and let you in without you having to wait your turn!"

I had a few questions. "What in the world is a *chuppah*? What's a *kesubah*? And what do I have to do? Does it hurt?" Neither Baruch nor I knew then what we know now, that a Jewish wedding is one of the most wonderful and sublime things that exist in this world. Hashem was giving it to us, innocent Jewish children, who were raised without knowledge of what it means to be a Jew; children who had never heard of Hashem and of His connection to the Jewish People. We were dry bones beginning to revive. The man at the consulate recommended that we ask our local *shul* if we could make the *chuppah* there. We called the *shul* in Odessa and the *shul* in Kiev, the capital of Ukraine. Both responses were the same: "We can only make a *chuppah* for couples who have a civil marriage." But since we weren't able to have a civil marriage, the answer was "No."

There was only one option left. The Israeli representatives had said to us, "Don't you dare go to the main Synagogue in Moscow: it is full of KGB informers. Instead, go to the Chabad *Shul* in Marina Roshcha (one of Moscow's districts). It's the only place that the Israelis will go to. They will help you."

The Marina Roshcha *Shul* was the first *shul* that I had ever entered. It was a small wooden building painted light blue with a white wooden Magen David under the triangular roof. When I stepped into this old synagogue, we felt as if we had gone back to a different era, some 150 to 200 years ago. There were elderly men with grey beards and crinkly faces sitting along old, worn tables. Their heads were covered with faded yarmulkes and their clothes were old and tattered. They looked like beggars as they quickly gulped down the warm soup that was being served to them. A group of Chassidim, who looked as if they had just stepped out of a Chagall painting, were dancing in a circle. A tall chassid with a curly, fiery red beard, black kartuz hat and stripped grey vest from under which protruded woolen *tzitzis*, dragged my groom into their circle. In a moment, Baruch joined their dance and, thanks to his beard, he fit in perfectly. We asked the chassidim what was going on, and were puzzled by their response. They were celebrating yesterday's *Melave Malka- Motzaei Shabbos* celebration, which had extended into Sunday evening...

There we were introduced to Rabbi Dovid Karpov. He listened attentively to our story, asked some questions, and then told us that it's not even a question: he'd make a *chuppah* for us, even though it was against the law. He explained, "It's important to me what Hashem wants. I do not care about government policies."

He handed me a package of what appeared to be pictures, held together with a rubber band. But it was a book, a seditious book on *Taharas Hamishpacha*. At that time, religious books were still taboo in the Soviet Union. A person could be sent to jail for self-publishing a book, or even for using Xerox to copy any kind of printed material. All copier machines were under the close supervision of KGB agents and one needed a special permit to use them. Rabbi Karpov told me that I must be very careful with this book. If I would lose even one of its pages, the Rabbi and the other people who were involved in its publication, as well as myself, could get into serious trouble. To tell you the truth, I was intrigued by this whole cloak and dagger thing…

Rabbi Karpov told me to return home and read this book carefully. If I agreed to follow all of its instructions, I should call the Rebbetzin to make an appointment to immerse in a *mikvah* and set the wedding date.

I returned home and started reading. But the moment I read the words "pure" and "impure," which, to me, sounded like "clean" and "unclean," I became annoyed. "Who is impure? Me?!! What?... They want to say I'm dirty? That I don't know how to take care of myself?!! These are medieval prejudices! It's unfair! I'm a modern woman in modern times, not in the Middle Ages!" I didn't realize that those terms referred to the spiritual sphere. The state of spiritual impurity had its source in a natural physiological process and had nothing to do with me as a person.

But although my feelings were hurt, I decided to read the book until the end. After all, I did want to get married. What did I have to lose by going to the *mikvah* that one time?

Shortly after setting a date with Rebbetzin Karpov, the Soviet Union's one and only news radio channel made a strange announcement: "The rumors that on February 4th a nationwide pogrom will take place against the Jews is false." This was shocking news. Although everyone took it seriously, Jews and non-Jews interpreted it differently. The non-Jews accepted it as an open call to action, while the Jews decided to keep a low profile and even not to send their children to school on that date.

For us, however, February 4th, 1990, had a special significance. It was our wedding date! Our guests called to say they weren't coming, but we were so excited about our *chuppah* that we could care less. Suddenly, we were no longer afraid. The darkness of the Soviet Empire had no power over us anymore.

Back then, when we were still in Moscow, we hitched a ride with a Russian officer in full uniform. In Russia, it's common etiquette for a man to remove his hat upon entering a building or a car, so when Baruch got into the car, his snow-covered hat came off, but his kippah remained! Our driver was more than a little surprised! Throughout the trip, the driver was completely silent, but every so often he glanced at us through the rear view mirror. We could see his scowl, but he saw our proud faces and victorious smiles. Our souls were shining, and no one, not even a scary-looking officer, could extinguish this flame!

Our *chuppah* took place outside, in the *shul*"s backyard, between snowdrifts. I circled my groom under a velvet *chuppah* canopy. It was so cold that I wore heavy boots and a brown sheepskin coat over my white wedding gown. We were surrounded by people we had never met before. For many of them this was the first time they were present at a *chuppah*. All the guests held lit candles, so our *chuppah* canopy was surrounded by a shining sea of singular flames. I looked up and saw the velvety blue sky full of sparkling stars. I'm sure our eyes were shining too.

Our wedding's Hebrew date was *Yud Shevat*, it was the fortieth anniversary of Rebbe Yosef Yitzchak's (the sixth Lubavicher Rebbe) passing, and the thirty-ninth anniversary of the day our Rebbe, Rabbi Menachem Mendel Schneerson, became a Rebbe. As the radio had predicted (unknowingly though), there was no pogrom. Our *chuppah* was the first Jewish wedding ceremony that Rabbi Karpov had arranged. His own *chuppah* had been just the year before.

Little did we know that twenty- five years later, in S.Francisco, my husband and I would have the privilege to meet Rabbi Karpov again. This time, we were able to show him our boys with yarmulkes and our girls dressed modestly, all of them receiving a proper Jewish education. He saw pictures from our oldest daughter's *chuppah*, which took place on the steps leading to Chabad Headquarters on 770 Eastern Parkway. She is married to a man whose great-grandfather was among those who built the little wooden *shul* in Marina Roshcha and who sacrificed his own life to keep Yiddishkeit in Soviet Russia.Twenty-five years after our *chuppah*, the circle was completed: now it was my turn to hand Rabbi Karpov the book, a legally printed book on *Taharas Hamishpacha*, written by me...This is the book you are holding right now.

The Special Virtue of the Women

We are presently standing at the end of the exile and are very close to the ultimate redemption, may it be speedily in our days. At this time, the merits of Jewish women are revealed in an even more palpable manner, as it is written:

"For the L-rd has created a new thing on the earth: a woman shall encircle man" (Yirmiyahu 31:21).

This refers to the virtues of the Jewish woman.

In spiritual sources, a woman possesses special higher qualities that will soon be revealed in the true and complete redemption.

This is why even now there is a custom for the bride to circle the groom under the wedding canopy.

The manner of encompassing in a circle also alludes to an everlasting building, which – like a circle – has no end.

The Basics of Family Purity

There are many books on the laws of keeping the *mitzvah* of *Taharas Hamishpacha*. There is a list of recommended reading at the end of this book. Although a book is good for reference, it is highly recommended to learn the laws of Family Purity from an experienced *madricha – mikvah* consultant. Contact your local Chabad House to find a *madricha* in your area.

This chapter will give you a general picture of the preparations necessary for immersing in the *mikvah*. **But please note that this information is not sufficient to properly observe this *mitzvah*.**

Jewish law forbids a husband and wife from having marital relations or any physical contact with each other when the wife is in the *niddah*[1] state. This is generally during the time of her actual period, which lasts from five to seven days, plus an additional seven days, known as the "seven clean days." At the end of this minimum of twelve to fourteen day period (depending upon the individual woman), the menstruant (known as a *niddah*) must immerse herself in a kosher *mikvah* and recite a special blessing in which she praises G-d for sanctifying us with His commandments and commanding us concerning immersion (*tevilla*h).

---

1. *Niddah* - a woman becomes a *niddah* when she is aware that blood has come from her womb, whether it is due to menstruation, childbirth or any other reason. It is not necessary for the woman to witness the flow of blood itself; it is sufficient for her to notice a stain that has indications of having originated in her womb.

Once a woman becomes *niddah,* she remains in that state until she immerses in a kosher *mikvah,* even if many years elapse. Therefore, a woman who no longer menstruates due to pregnancy, menopause, or a hysterectomy and did not immerse in a *mikvah* after the last time she became *niddah,* still remains in that state. She must separate from her husband for five days, make a *Hefsek Taharah,* count the seven clean days with *bedikos,* and then, after making the proper preparations, immerse in a kosher *mikvah.*

A post-menopausal woman who is still *niddah* usually goes to the *mikvah* only once, after separating from her husband for five days, making a *Hefsek Taharah,* counting seven days with *bedikos,* and making all the necessary preparations prior to her immersion. In most cases, she will remain *t'horah* (pure) for the rest of her life in her present marriage.

1. Hefsek Taharah

A *Hefsek Taharah* marks the end of menstruation and the beginning of the seven day count that precedes immersion in the *mikvah.*

The *Hefsek Taharah* is a simple internal examination. The examination should be carried out before sunset on the day that her period ends, provided there has been a minimum of five days from the onset of menstruation. (Even if a woman's period lasts less than five days, she must still wait a minimum of five days from the onset before examining herself.)

How do you make a *Hefsek Taharah*?

1. Wash your whole body (preferably take a bath) before making the check. If that is not possible, wash the intimate area only.

2. Wrap a piece of white soft natural fabric (100% cotton) 7X8 cm or 2.76"X3.15" around your index finger. This piece of fabric is called the Ed *Bedikah*. You can purchase packages of pre-washed, pre-cut Ed *Bedikah* cloths, from your madricha. These packages are also usually sold at the *mikvah*. (In Israel you can find Edei *Bedikah* in many pharmacies and supermarkets.)

Insert the finger with the fabric into the vagina, as deeply as you can, and with a rotational motion examine all internal creases and folds. After removing the fabric, carefully examine it by daylight. If the secretion found on the fabric is of a "clean" color: white, yellow, or green, then the *Hefsek Taharah* check is successful. Even a minute speck of blood makes this check "unclean". If the secretion on the fabric is a questionable color and it is unclear whether it's "clean" or not, it is necessary to ask a competent Orthodox Rabbi. (You can send your test and be answered in a completely discreet way. There is no need to meet with the Rabbi personally, and this service is free of charge).

If you were unsuccessful in making a "clean" check prior to sunset, you should repeat the check the following day. After a successful *Hefsek Taharah* examination, you should wear clean, solid white underwear.

Upon completing the *Hefsek Taharah*, there is a custom to make another check called the Moch Dachuk. Another piece of clean white fabric (an Ed *Bedikah* cloth) is inserted into the vagina and left there from before sunset until nightfall. The color of the removed fabric should be observed under the same rules as the *Hefsek Taharah*. A woman that has any problem doing this check should consult a Rabbi.

2. The Seven Clean Days

The counting of the Seven Clean Days begins on the morning following a successful *Hefsek Taharah* check. During these seven days you should check yourself twice each day: in the morning and before sunset, in the same way that you checked yourself with the *Hefsek Taharah*. If for whatever reason, you missed one of these checks, you may continue counting on condition that you performed at least a *Hefsek Taharah*, plus one check on the first and one check on the seventh day.

Throughout these seven clean days, you should wear solid white underwear and sleep on a solid white sheet.

3. Preparations for Immersion

The immersion is performed at the end of the seventh clean day, after the stars appear in the sky.

A very thorough cleaning of the entire body should precede the immersion. It's better to begin the preparations before sunset, after the second check of the seventh day.

Remove all jewelry, eye glasses, contact lenses, hair pins, dentures, bandages, etc. Thoroughly remove all traces of nail polish and makeup. Cut your fingernails and toenails, brush and floss your teeth, clean your ears, nose, eyes etc. A full list of preparations can be found in the *mikvah*.

Contact an Orthodox Rabbi if it is important for you to keep your manicure/pedicure.

It's important to take a bath. The water should be warm and pleasant. Thoroughly clean your entire body and shampoo your hair. After completing the bath, rinse in a shower. All hair is to be combed. You should examine yourself to make sure that there is nothing that could come between your body and the *mikvah* water (such as loose hair, a hangnail, splinter, etc).

A thorough, meticulous washing of your entire body with warm water, combing of your hair, and examination of your body are mandatory before immersion.

4. Immersion in the Mikvah

The idea of immersion is to gain ritual purity, which goes beyond intellectual comprehension.

Although certain commandments can be explained by logic, such as giving money to the poor, or respecting another person's property, the *mitzvah* of *Taharas Hamishpacha* is a *Chok* - a type of Divine commandment whose meaning is beyond human comprehension. We keep this *mitzvah* without understanding it, with pure faith that our Creator and Father is interested in our wellbeing and knows what's best for us, His creations.

A *Balanit* (*mikvah* lady) must be present during your immersion in the *mikvah*. The *Balanit* is a Jewish woman who is well-versed in the laws of immersion. She will observe your immersion and make sure that it is according to Halacha (Jewish law). She will also be happy to assist you when necessary.

How should you immerse?

In order to purify yourself, immerse your entire body in the water of the *mikvah*, so that not even one hair is above the water's surface. Stand in a position in which the water is surrounding you on all sides, and reaches every place of your body at once. Each time you purify yourself in the *mikvah*, in addition to returning to your previous state of purity, you are also reaching a higher spiritual level.

Stand in the *mikvah* (the depth of the water in the *mikvah* is about 120 cm. or 3.9 feet). Be relaxed, hold your hands outward separating your fingers and stand with your legs apart. Your eyes and mouth should be gently, not tightly, closed.

Bend your knees slightly and lean forward, so your body, including all your hair, is entirely under the water. After the first immersion, return to a standing position, place your hands across your body under your chest, not touching it with your palms, and say the blessing:

BARUCH ATA, ADO-NAY, ELO-HEINU, MELECH HAOLAM,
ASHER KID'SHANU B'MITZVOTAV VETZIVANU AL HATVILLAH.

This means: "Blessed are You, Lord our G-d, King of the universe, who has sanctified us with His commandments, and commanded us regarding immersion."

Right after you say the blessing, you immerse 2 more times. After each correct immersion, the *mikvah* lady will say:"Kosher", and HaShem, approving, affirms:"Kosher!"

After immersing in the *mikvah*, you are pure and permitted to be intimate with your husband again!

The gates of Heaven are opened for you at the moment of your immersion. Use this special time to pray to the Creator for yourself, your family and friends, and for all of the Jewish people. At this moment you have a special power to bless others! Bless everyone with all they need.

After the immersion you will feel pure, renewed, and at peace.

Wishing you good luck!

Glossary

Abba (father Heb.)

Alter Rebbe- Rabbi Shneur Zalman of Liadi (1745-1812)— founder of Chabad.

Am Segulah- i.e. the Jewish people. Treasured Nation.

Am Yisrael- the Jewish people. Nation of Israel.

Apirion- canopy, *Chuppah*.

B'ezrat Hashem- with G-d's help.

Baba- a Sephardic mystic.

Bedikah, Bedikos (pl.)- self-performed internal examination of the vaginal canal performed with a special clean white cloth. *Bedikos* are a necessary to obtain Purity.

Bli Ayin Hara- "without the evil eye".

Brachah- Beracha- blessing.

Bris- the Jewish rite of circumcision.

Chabad- Lubavitch Chabad- an Orthodox Jewish Chassidic movement.

Chas v'shalom- G-d forbid.

Chassid, Chassidim (pl.)- meaning "pious"- follower of Chassidism.

Chassidishe – Chassidic.

Chassidus- Chassidic philosophy- branch of Orthodox Judaism.

Cheshbon HaNefesh- "soul accounting", - introspection.

Chinuch Al Taharas Hakodesh- Torah education (chinuch), Jewish education in a pure and sacred manner.

Chukei Retzonecho- statutes of *Hashem's* Will.

Chuppah- a canopy under which a Jewish couple stand during their Jewish wedding ceremony.

Dvar Torah- a Torah lesson

Edim- *Bedikah* cloth- specially cut pieces of clean white fabric needed to make *Hefsek Taharah* and *bedikos.* See *Bedikah*

Eis Ratzon- an auspicious time.

Eretz Yisrael- the Land of Israel.

Farbrengen- a Chabad Chassidic gathering consisting of explanations of different Torah subjects, Chassidic stories, singing chassidic melodies and include refreshments.

Gemara- the component of the Talmud comprising rabbinical analysis of and commentary on the Mishnah.

Geulah- Final Redemption from *Golus* (Exile).- Jewish principle of faith, the purpose for which HaShem created the world. We believe that Moshiach will come and redeem us from exile very soon in our days. The Lubavitcher Rebbe said that our generation merited to be the last generation of Exile and the first generation of Redemption.

Hachnasas (Haknassas) Sefer Torah - a happy ceremony of presenting a new Sefer Torah (Torah scroll) to synagogue.

Halacha/ Halachos- Jewish religious laws derived from Written and Oral Torah given to the Jewish people on mountain Sinai.

Halachic- according to *Halacha.*

Harei at mekudeshet li b'tabaat zu k'dat Moshe v'Yisrael- these words are said by the groom when placing the ring on his bride's finger. They mean that the woman is now wedded to him, according to the laws of the Torah. It is part of the traditional chuppah ceremony.

Hashem, Hashem Elokeinu, Hashem Yisbarach- Lord, our G-d, Blessed G-d

Hashgachah Pratis- Divine Providence.

Hatzlacha- success.

Hefsek Taharah- A special internal examination with the *Bedikah* cloth (see *Bedikah*) to show that all bleeding from the uterus has ceased. After completing the Hefsek Taharah a woman can begin the seven day count that precedes immersion in the mikvah.

Igrot Kodesh - the collection of the Lubavitcher Rebbe's correspondence. So far, 30 volumes of Rebbe's letters have been printed.

Ima- mother

K'dat Moshe v'Yisrael- according to the law of Moses and Yisrael- applies to traditional Jewish marriage.

Kallah - Jewish bride.

Kartuz- a hat with small visor.

Kashrus- Jewish dietary laws.

Kedushah- Holiness.

Kesivah Vechasimah Tovah L'Shana Tova Umesukah, (a good inscribing and sealing for a good and sweet year)- a traditional greeting before Rosh Hashanah- Jewish New Year.

Kesubah - Jewish marriage contract.

Kittel- a white robe worn by Jewish men on Yom Kippur. According to many traditions a groom wears a kittel on his wedding day.

Klal Yisrael - Jewish People.

Kosher- Kosher according to Jewish dietary laws.

L'chaim- "To Life"- a toast used in drinking to a person's health or well-being.

Levush- a garment, in this book- a garment of the soul.

Loshon Kodesh- the holy tongue i.e. Hebrew.

Lubavitcher- a member of Chabad Chassidic movement founded by Alter Rebbe. Lubavitch- a town in

Belarus that was the center of the Chabad movement.

Mamash- - really, precisely, exactly. The use of word Mamash means you should understand whatever has been said, is meant literally.

Mazal Tov – Congratulations, good luck

Melave Malka- a meal at the end of the Shabbat, on Saturday night.

Mesirus nefesh- self-sacrifice.

Mezuzah, Mezuzos(pl.)- a piece of parchment inscribed with specific verses of Torah that is affixed to the doorposts.

Mikvah, Mikvaot(pl.)- means "gathering" or "collection" in Hebrew, denoting a collection of water to one place. A spring-fed pool, an ocean or a lake, are naturally occurring mikvahs. Generally however, the mikvah has almost always been indoors, allowing users the privacy and comfort required. A modern-day mikvah looks like a miniature swimming pool.

Minyan- a minimum of ten Jewish men over the age of 13 required for certain religious obligations.

Mitzvah- G-d's Commandment.

Moshiach- Messiah, The Messianic Redemption will be ushered in by a person, a human leader, a descendant of King David, who will rebuild the Holy Temple in Jerusalem. In every generation there is a scion of the House of David who has the potential to be the Moshiach. With Moshiach comes *Geulah*, the Final Redemption.

Motzoei Shabbos- an evening immediately following Shabbat.

Shabbos Hagodol- a Shabbos preceding a Holiday of Passover.

Nachas- pride or gratification, especially at the achievements of one's offspring.

Nasi Hador- Leader of the generation, the Rebbe, who is bonded with the souls of all the Jews of his generation, the head of the Jewish people.

Niggun- Chassidic tune, melody.

Nshei Chabad- Chabad women organization.

Otzar- tank of water- a part of the mikvah's construction.

Parnassah- livelihood.

Psak Halacha- Halachic ruling.

Rambam- Maimonides, Rabbi Moshe ben Maimon, (1135- 1204), one of the greatest Jewish thinker, Talmudist, and codifier in the Middle Ages

Rebbe- here referring to the Lubavitcher Rebbe, Menachem Mendel Schneerson

Rebbetzin- Rabbi's wife

Refuah Shleimah- complete recovery

Segulah, segulos (pl.)- a remedy, a good sign. An action that will lead to a change in one's future for good.

Sefer- a holy book

Shaliach- member of the Chabad Hasidic movement who is sent by the Rebbe to promulgate Judaism and Chassidism in locations around the world.

Shalom bayis- domestic harmony.

Shavuos- Jewish holiday which commemorates the anniversary of the day G-d gave the Torah to the entire Jewish nation

Shefa - overflowing abundance

Shidduch- a Jewish arranged marriage.

Shiur, shiurim (pl.)- a class, study session on Jewish tradition.

Shiva nekiyim- the seven clean days that are a prerequisite to immersion in the mikvah.

Shul- Synagogue

Sichos Hashavuah- Chabad weekly pamphlet distributed in Israel.

Siyatta DiShmaya- Aramaic "with the help of Heaven".

Sofer Sta"m- a Jewish scribe who writes Torah scrolls, tefillin and mezuzahs.

Taharah- ritual purity.

Taharas Hamishpacha- Jewish laws of family purity.

Tahor- a ritual state of purity.

Tallis- Jewish prayer shawl.

Tanya- written by Shneur Zalman of Liadi, is the main work of the Chabad philosophy.

Tefillin- phylacteries.

Tehillim- the book of Psalms.

Tevilla- immersion.

Tinok SheNishba- literally "captured infant", is a Talmudical term that refers to a Jew who lives a secular life inadvertently, as a result of having been raised without an appreciation for the thought and practices of Judaism.

Tishrei- First month of the Jewish year. We celebrate Rosh Hashanah, Yom Kippur, and Sukkos during this month.

Toras Hachassidus- Chassidism.

Tzaddikim- righteous.

Tzedakah- Charity.

Tzitzis- the fringes on the corners of the tallit.

Ulpan- Hebrew immersion classes.

Yechi…- short for *Yechi Adoneinu, Moreinu veRabeinu Melech Hamoshiach LeOlam vaEd*- "Long live our master, teacher and Rebbe, King Moshiach, forever!"

Yiddishkeit- the Jewish way of life with its customs and practices.

Yud Shevat- 10th of Jewish month Shevat.

Zayin Neki'im- The seven days of cleanliness.

List of Mikvah consultants:

Shulamit Pape, Brooklyn, NY **(347) 909- 0879**

Liel Maximov, Brooklyn, NY **(347) 771- 0221**

Leah Yechielov, Brooklyn, NY **(917) 754- 3700**

Tziporah Vogel, Brooklyn, NY **(347) 645- 1436**

Luba Perlov, S.Jose, CA **(408) 735- 5948 PT**

Mattie Pil, S.Francisco, CA **(415) 933- 4310 PT**

Bibliography

1. "The Power of Mikvah" based on Rabbi Raskin's audio lecture

2. Rebbe's Letter taken from the book by Rabbi S.Z. Lesches «Understanding Mikvah», Kolel Menachem

3. "A Marriage Saved", "Immersion with Self-Sacrifice", "Clear Eyes", "Jewish Legacy" and "The Special Virtue of the Women" and excerpts of translations of Rebbe's talks taken from the book "A Happy Home" by Rabbi Ze'ev Ritterman, Torah-Or

Recommended reading:

"A Guide to Family Purity" by Rabbi Yisroel Yosef HaCohen Hendel

"Kitzur Dinei Taharah" in Hebrew with English translation Rabbis Y Loebenstein and S.B. Wineberg

"A Happy Home", The Lubavitcher Rebbe on Marital Harmony by Rabbi Ze'ev Ritterman

With praise and gratitude to *Hashem Yisbarach*, and thanks to the Rebbe's blessings and constant guidance!

יחי אדוננו מורנו ורבינו מלך המשיח לעולם ועד

With gratitude to our donors:

The production of this book was made possible by the generous donations of caring people!
May Hashem bless them with an abundance of blessings in material and spiritual matters.
May He listen to their prayers and help those who need, find their soul mates, healthy children being born, true Jewish Chassidic *Nachas* from offspring, physical and spiritual health and prosperity!

&Brodkin Aharon & Maya, Hadera, Israel

&Chrinevitzkiy Alex & Sarah, Netanya, Israel

&Feikin Konstantin & Dina in honor of their son Yonathan, Netanya, Israel

&Geishtadt Yoel & Sheyna, Hadera, Israel

&Gvilli Ruti, Netanya, Israel

&Hendel Rabbi Shneur Zalman Eliyahu & Rebbetzin Chaya Rachel, Tzfat, Israel

&Hershovitch Shaul and Rinah in honor of their kids שיחיו

&Kapustin Julia in honor of her son, Vitaliy, Netanya, Israel

&Perlo Gennadiy & Peninah, Pardes Hana, Israel for elevation of the souls of Dmitry ben Zusov Kottler ז"ל and Maya bat Semiyon Kottler ז"ל-their souls should merit that their offspring will bring up Jewish families

&Perlov Baruch & Luba, S.Jose, CA, US

&Riss Eliyahu & Anna Michal, Birobidzhan, Russia

&Roitman Lipa Chanina & Chaya Rachel, Netanya, Israel

&Rosenshtein Mordehai & Ruchama, Netanya, Israel- in honor of our Rebbe, King Moshiach!

&Shvartsman Aharon Ilan & Efrat, Tzfat, Israel, good news soon *mamosh*!

&Shvarts Avraham & Tamar in honor of their sons Mordechai and Menachem Mendel, Holon, Israel

&Shvartsman Marina for complete recovery of her daughter Emily Rivkah, Netanya, Israel

&Shvartsman Yakov & Raya in honor of their daughter Yaarah, Hadera, Israel

&Vasserman Nechama, Akko, Israel

&Wurmser Yehudith Batia, Petach Tikva, Israel, for the elevation of the soul of her grandmother, Kreindel Weissmann daughter of Rabbi Moshe Levi זצ"ל

&Zaitzev Alex & Orah, Tzefat, Israel

&Zelig Yehudith Bnei Brak, Israel

Made in the USA
San Bernardino, CA
16 October 2015

«And G-d made the rib... into a woman»
(Bereshit 2:12). Rav Chisdah said: «This
teaches us that The Holy One, Blessed
Be He, endowed an additional level of
understanding to the woman more than
to the man.»

(Babylonian Talmud, Niddah 45b)

ISBN 9781517124946

9000

9 781517 124946